NAKED
FILMMAKING:

HOW TO MAKE A FEATURE-LENGTH FILM
- *WITHOUT A CREW* -
FOR $10,000 OR LESS

BY

MIKE CARROLL

ONE-MAN FILMMAKER
WRITER
PRODUCER
DIRECTOR
CINEMATOGRAPHER
EDITOR

BOOKS BY MIKE CARROLL

Breaking Into TV News: How To Get A Job & Excel
As A TV Reporter-Photographer

FILMS AVAILABLE ON DVD
AND AS DIGITAL DOWNLOADS TO OWN OR RENT

Dog Soldiers: The Dogumentary

Year

Nightbeats

NAKED FILMMAKING: HOW TO MAKE A FEATURE-LENGTH FILM—WITHOUT A CREW—FOR $10,000 OR LESS. © 2010 by Mike Carroll. All rights reserved. Printed in the United States of America. No part of this book may be used or reproduced in any manner whatsoever without permission except in the case of brief quotations embodied in critical articles or reviews.

mikecarrollfilms.com

ISBN-13: 978-1-450-51026-4
ISBN-10: 1-450-51026-4

First Edition: March 2010

Revised: June 2012

Dedicated to my amazing wife
Bonnie,
who unhesitatingly encouraged me to jump
into the digital revolution and has supported
every computer and camera investment along
the way and always been honest with me
whether an idea did or didn't work. Not many
people can claim that kind of support in their
partner. I still find it pretty amazing myself.
Everyone tells me I'm a lucky man. But then, I
knew that already.

UP FRONT NOTE TO READERS:

"Dramatic Films"

This is my term for all narrative (non-documentary) films that involve scripts and actors, whether they're drama, comedy, musical, action, sci-fi, whatever.

Also, this book only deals with how to make a movie and not the wheeler-dealer aspects of money-raising, deal-making, negotiating, profit participation or points. Although, if someone promises to pay you in profit points in lieu of cash don't think twice, get up and walk away. That's because in the movie business nothing ever goes into profit. Companies keep cranking out film after film that pull in loads and loads of bread, yet all the accountants' books show nothing but red. In spite of this bookkeeping anomaly wheeler-dealer producers and executives still wind up with new cars, big houses and heated pools.

Table of Contents

First Movie Memory

A huge profile of a man with blond hair and blue eyes stares intently at a burning match. The man's mouth wrinkles in a bemused smile and blows out the flame. In the blink of an eye we're transported to an expanse of desert.

Two men in Arab robes stand caked in sand and dust, parched from thirst, on the edge of madness. Then from out of the wilderness comes the blast of a ship's horn. Beyond the crest of sand dunes appear the smoke stacks of a steam ship. The two men race up a sandy slope to behold the rich, blue waters of the Suez Canal.

The same blue-eyed man astride a horse leads a thunderous charge into a tattered, defeated army of retreating Turks.

Finally, the blond-haired man stares off into nothing as he's driven out of the desert.

This was my first movie going memory. I was seven or eight and my parents had taken my brother and me to see *Lawrence Of Arabia*. To be honest, I didn't understand anything on the screen. But I loved every frame. It was a defining moment. I've never been the same since.

GETTING NAKED

na·ked film·mak·er (nā-kəd film-mā-kər) *noun*
a: an artist of motion pictures responsible for all
aspects of motion picture production; **b:** a writer-
producer-director-cinematographer-soundman-editor
of a film; **c:** an auteur who makes a film without a
crew and is solely responsible for the production
quality, *as in having no one else to blame.*

Why "Naked Filmmaking?"

WHY? ARE YOU KIDDING? BECAUSE I WANT THIS BOOK TO SELL. I want people to find this on Amazon and Google. Because *Naked Filmmaking* will get a bigger draw than calling it *Digital Filmmaking, Camcorder Cinema or How To Make Movies (That Nobody's Gonna See)*. Besides, you found it, didn't you?

Another thing, this is not a book about how to make porn. Sorry to disappoint. Though you can certainly apply these filmmaking techniques to do that. And if you do be sure to send me a DVD.

I believe artists who take their work seriously stand naked in judgment before the audience every time their work is presented. I feel this every time someone watches a film that I've written, directed, photographed, edited, recorded most if not all the sound, authored the DVD, and perhaps even played at a film festival out of my laptop and onto the screen. Every time someone watches one of my films I am exposing all of my talents to be accepted or rejected. Hence, Naked Filmmaking.

I've made three feature films: *Dog Soldiers, Year* and *Nightbeats*. All have played in film festivals. All are available on DVD. All have been made using the methods that I'll share with you in this book.

Back in the pre-digital day when making an independent film meant 16mm, synchronized sound, editing on a Moviola, an audio remix and a one-pass print of the film there was no way around the $20K-$30K investment. That's *if* you knew what you were doing. Nowadays there is no reason why you can't make a short or feature film or music video for $10,000. If you already have a state-of-the-art computer in front of you it could be less than that.

People say things to me like, "You must really like making movies. It must be a lot of fun." I always say that if you're having fun making a movie then you aren't working hard enough. Filmmaking takes a lot of work and a lot of time. I'd rather be out walking the dogs or watching a movie. But if you have a movie in your head and you want other people to see it, the only way to make that happen is to put a lot of time and a lot of work into it. Nobody is going to make your movie for you.

Every time I make a film it's from a script that I write. Every shot is one that I shoot. Almost every element of sound is something that I recorded. I direct the actors, though I strive as much as possible to leave them alone to do what they want to do. I edit every frame of footage, listening to every line, scrutinizing every facial reaction, every long shot, medium shot and close-up, deciding exactly how the movie will finally look and play.

There's a business phrase that's gotten lots of traction, "Doing more with less." I do everything with next to nothing. I'm continually baffled by people making no-budget films who believe they need to have a full-size crew made up entirely of volunteers with little or no experience who ultimately only confuse and distract.

I also design the posters, maintain the website, author the DVDs and design the DVD labels and box art.

Until you're into the realm of filmmaking where you have financing and budgets and can hire experienced professionals the only person you can count on to get done what you want when you want and to your standards is you.

Frank Capra said it best. Recognizing that films made by committees came out as confused muddles, he created his own motto, "One man, one film." He came up with the story, worked with a writer, produced and directed the picture and, unprecedented for that era of studio filmmaking, oversaw the editing through to final cut.

Don't ask someone else to do what you can do yourself.

Register Your Name As Your Website

THE FIRST THING A FILMMAKER OR ANY ARTIST OR PROFESSIONAL should do is to register their name as a .com for the domain name of their website. Names have value and you should register yours today so that you own it. As you develop as a filmmaker and your star begins to rise you want people to be able to easily find you on the web. This has nothing to do with Facebook or Myspace or any of the other social networking sites, which are useful as well.

Several established directors maintain their own sites and blogs:

Kevin Smith	kevinsmith.com
David Lynch	davidlynch.com
Alex Cox	alexcox.com

Francis Ford Coppola's company is called American Zoetrope, but American Zoetrope is not as well known as Francis Ford Coppola. If Francis Ford Coppola were starting out today I'll bet you he'd be blogging and selling DVDs of his films at francisfordcoppola.com.

Kevin Smith's book, *My Boring Ass Life: The Uncomfortably Candid Diary of Kevin Smith,* was compiled from a blog page on his site. Alex Cox has posted .pdf files of most of his scripts, both produced and unproduced, for people to read, as well as a finance page where people can invest in his films.

Look at all the production company names you see at the beginning of a movie these days. Can anyone remember any of them? However, people do know Steven Speilberg, George Lucas, Quentin Tarantino, Joel & Ethan Coen—it's their *names* that have earned value.

By the time I caught onto this my name had already been taken so I registered mikecarrollfilms.com. For a time my company was licensed as The Garage Filmworks, because I do my editing in a converted garage. But no one is going to remember that. I've recently dropped that name and have re-registered simply as mikecarrollfilms.com. I believe that almost all business in the future will be driven by the Internet, so whenever anyone hears about my work in films or books or anything, I want them to easily be able to find me through my name on a web search.

Make Your Own Film—Build Your Own Site

Just as I encourage filmmakers to take possession of their films and eliminate the middlemen, I encourage you to take possession of your website as well.

Web design software is constantly getting easier and friendlier to use. There's plenty of simple software and on-line web-building sites that can help demystify the process to just a couple clicks of a mouse and the dragging of .jpegs or QuickTime files from your desktop onto a blank page. So have no fear. Dive in now and start getting comfortable with the process.

I started my site a few years ago. I was a bit intimidated at the outset because I'm not a terribly tech-savvy guy. I don't know anything about designing software, computer language, what Linux or UNIX is, and I hate trying to follow complicated directions in computer instruction manuals. To help overcome my Internet fears, and being a converted and confirmed Mac guy, I signed up for a .Mac account, which makes creating a website so simple that I haven't even had to read the instructions. On the flip side, it had the long-winded address of http://web.mac.com/mikecarrollfilms. Nobody on the planet was ever going to find that. So I went to an external server, registered the domain name mikecarrollfilms.com and set it up so that whenever someone clicked on that web address they were forwarded to the .Mac site. This way everything was kept under one roof and I didn't have lots of separate web sites to maintain.

I also registered the names of my films, year-movie.com and nightbeats-movie.com, and have them forwarded to mikecarrollfilms.com so people can be introduced to those and any other projects I'm working on.

Just as the Internet is constantly changing and evolving, I've had to change and evolve as well. I currently am using WordPress and have signed up with an Internet provider who sets up all of my various domain names with URL Forwarding so that everything links back to mikecarrollfilms.com.

Make It Easy For People To Find You On The Web

Once your film is finished you're going to be wiped out physically and mentally and not ready, willing, interested or strong enough to start learning something new.

The biggest reason to maintain your own site is to keep it updated regularly. This allows you to:

- Post a blog about your film's progress
- Post pictures from the set and frame blowups from scenes
- Post video clips of scenes, a trailer, making-of videos and a blog
- Keep up the morale of your actors and any crew and investors you may have
- Spread the word about your project on Facebook and Twitter and any other social networking site that's out there
- Try to develop any buzz you can for your film
- Keep people coming back

People come back to websites to see what's new. Post new things to your site every day or every couple of days to get people hooked and keep them coming back. Generating buzz is priceless and can be so important toward getting your film accepted into festivals. By maintaining your site yourself and regularly posting updates you'll have a fully constructed website by the time you're announcing that your film's been accepted into a festival. A little work every couple of days will save mountains of work at the end.

Domain names are cheap. Buy your name and your film's title as domain names now.

The Importance Of The Blog

Filmmaking, cameras and computer technology is constantly evolving. Changing even faster is the Internet.

Since starting my own site a few years ago the basic website model consisting of the home page with various other pages linked to it has gone through a major shift to the blog-driven website. The blog page, which had been buried in the basic website, has now become the home page with all the other pages linked off from it. The motivating reason for this is to keep people coming back to your site on a regular, if not daily basis.

By having the blog page as the home page the first thing people see when they click on your site is your latest entry, hopefully posted within the past 48 hours, about you and your film's progress. And, perhaps, how they can participate.

Free open-source software like WordPress with ready-to-use downloadable templates is spearheading this movement. The independent filmmaker needs to stay relevant and up-to-date. You must stay on top of this wave or be swamped by it. I certainly intend to hang ten and surf on, both with this wave and wherever the next Internet tide takes me.

(Since starting this book over two years ago I've had to rewrite this section half a dozen times to keep it current. That's how fast the Internet and its users change.)

Why Do You Want To Make A Movie?

WHY SPEND A SIGNIFICANT PORTION OF YOUR SAVINGS OR CREDIT and every spare moment of your life for a year or more laboring on a movie that can be watched in an hour and a half? And why should complete strangers, not just your family and friends, want to watch it?

Search inside yourself. Be honest. Why do you want to make a movie? To be famous? Get rich? Be on the cover of *People*? Have a mansion in Beverly Hills? A Maserati? Enjoy sex with beautiful women? Or men? Or both? To be admired? Respected? Interviewed?

Is it therapy? To explore something in your life? Your childhood? Your sexuality? Prove something? To your family who doesn't understand you? To your father who's always belittled you? To your mother who only wants a grandchild?

All of these reasons are perfectly valid. Now, are you ready for the real challenge? Go out and make a Good Movie.

REALITY: The odds are stacked against you.

When I make a movie I have essentially no money. I can't afford any stars to sell it. I can't afford to rent locations. It's just me.

THE CHALLENGE: Make a movie that stands on it's own without any excuses.

Many people say, "I just need to make something so I can get an investor to give me money for a real movie."

If that's how you feel about moviemaking then don't even try. Money is not going to make a good movie. Walk down the aisles of any video store and you'll see title after title that you've never heard of. Of the ones you have heard of, how many were worth the hour and a half or two hours they took to watch?

TRUTH: Any movie that turns out to be any good at all is a miracle.

If you try to make a film in the no-budget D.I.Y. (Do-It-Yourself) method that I'm going to map out it's important that you enjoy the journey because independent moviemaking offers very few rewards beyond being proud of the film you make. Everybody with a camcorder is making a movie these days. Just click on Youtube. Every year film festivals receive thousands of film submissions, only to accept a handful. I spoke with a screener for Sundance who was given 75 movies and was required to watch every minute of them. At least twenty were Tarantino rip-offs. She found only five that she could recommend.

Afterwards, she thought people should have to get a license before they could make a film.

When was the last time you saw a movie that was still on your mind the next morning and that remained there for a few days or even a week after? Damn few. And what made it good? The actor? The story? The writer? The director? Or was it some intangible that made it stand out? There's a word for that. It's something that can't be bought. It is in fact priceless. It's called Art.

ADVICE FROM THE GUT: Don't let Fear get in your way.

In the Great Depression of the 1930s people were broken, giving up. Then Franklin Delano Roosevelt came along and told the country, "We have nothing to fear but fear itself."

Don't be afraid. Don't wait around for somebody to make your movie for you. Make your own movie. You'll spend some money. But you won't have to mortgage your house or raid your 401K. A credit card will do. One single credit card. You'll get a great camera, microphones, lights, a good computer. Five to ten thousand dollars to fulfill a dream. How many dreams can be bought for that?

If you've never made a movie before, your first film will very likely have much room for improvement. It might even stink. When it's all finished, you'll probably look back and realize all the things you'd do differently. That's okay, it's part of the learning process. Don't be afraid. You'll have the camera, the computer, the software. Several months or a year will have passed and a chunk of the credit card debt should be paid down.

Give it another try. Do it again.

> **FINANCIAL NOTE:** Don't charge all your production costs to your credit card, then only pay the monthly minimum. Send in two or three times the minimum. As much as you can. Pay down the principle. Don't destroy your credit rating over a movie.

> **BOTTOM LINE:** Don't count on your movie to win the lottery.

After *Year* played in San Francisco I got an inquiry from a producer's rep in L.A. asking to see the film. I mailed her a DVD and the following week she called. At some point in the conversation she asked how much our budget was.

"How much did it look like?"

"Oh, I don't know. A hundred and fifty thousand."

Then I told her.

"You did all that for *just* eighty thousand dollars?"

"No, eight. Eight thousand dollars."

"*Eight* thousand dollars? You made *that whole film* for just *eight thousand dollars?* How can anybody do that?"

It can be done.

Is It Art Or Artifice?

A NATURAL INCLINATION WHEN YOU FIRST START WRITING and making films is to mold them after the films and filmmakers that have influenced you. I certainly did with *Year* and *Nightbeats*, making them in the handheld, natural light style of Claude Lelouch's films and Michael Winterbottom's *Wonderland* and *In This World*.

Most wannabe filmmakers go out of their way to make their films look "Hollywood," copying lighting, camera setups, music, acting style, everything. So what?

Go to any Starbucks in L.A. and you can find film school grads who can crank that stuff out like nonfat lattes. The one thing Hollywood is always looking for is an "Original Voice." Copycats are as plentiful as blades of grass. It's the "Original Voice" who stands out from the pack.

Stupid Filmmaker Cliches

"I love making movies. It's the most fun! I never want to do anything else."

> TRUTH: They're not working hard enough.

"What I love about filmmaking is collaborating with other talented artists."

> TRUTH: I don't know what I'm doing so I need people to do it for me.

"Yeah, I'm gonna make a film and I'll let Sundance run it."

> TRUTH: Doesn't have a clue.

"If I'm going to be taken seriously I need a tripod, a camera dolly and a lighting kit."

> TRUTH: Your movie can't stand out if it looks like everybody else's.

"I've got a great script that's going to make a great film."

> TRUTH: By using "great" and other dynamic adjectives to describe themselves they are trying to convince you (and perhaps themselves) of their talent.

"I'm a very creative person and my real strength is finding creative solutions."

> ALERT: Beware of anybody who overuses the word "creative."

Nobody Wants To Read Your Script

"I've written a great screenplay that Hollywood will pay big bucks to make. Why should I ever consider spending my own money to make a movie out of my script when I can sell it and move to Beverly Hills?"

In any agency or production company office you'll find the walls lined with three-foot high stacks of scripts. Thousands and thousands of pages perfectly formatted in IBM Courier 10 that nobody wants to read. It's so much easier to watch a movie. Pop a DVD in a player and in thirty seconds they can tell whether someone knows how to make a movie or not.

The new industry trend is to let the film festival screeners wade through the thousands of submissions and weed out the home movies from the real movies. Those are the films to see and the filmmakers to talk to.

A script only has value if someone wants to make it. If you can't find someone who wants to make it, or someone even willing to read it, then it's time to try something else.

If the script you want to make is too expensive, write a script for a film you can afford to make, then try to get attention through film festivals to generate the interest to make your dream project.

You can read, research, talk, plan, write, pitch, dream, make trailers to seek investors and all that other crap. Henry Ford built his first car in his garage. There's nothing to hold you back from making your first film the same way. Time to fish or cut bait.

The Big Lie: You Need To Shoot On Film To Be Taken Seriously

IN THE WORLD OF NO-BUDGET FILMMAKING, where you are the bank, shooting 16mm or 35mm film is not an option. Shooting on film is a bottomless pit of production costs that will sink you faster than the Titanic.

If you've never shot anything before some people may advise you to look for a cinematographer. A cinematographer will tell you, "If you want to be taken seriously as a filmmaker you need to shoot on film, 16mm or 35mm." If you listen to him, make an appointment with a good tax attorney and begin preparing for bankruptcy.

The sad truth is that cinematographers are junkies. They shoot Kodak stock into their veins. You can find them hanging around the sidewalk outside Technicolor Labs trying to bum short ends for a quick fix. They need a rookie with deep pockets to fund their habit because, like all junkies, they need other people's money to cover their Jones.

They'll never mention films like *Open Water*, made by Chris Kentis and Laura Lau on Sony PD-150 camcorders that went on to a big Sundance premiere and nationwide blockbuster release, or *28 Days Later*, shot on Canon XL1 camcorders, and redefined the horror film.

A cinematographer will argue that you can economically shoot a feature film in 16mm or 35mm for $30,000. Your $30,000. He'll also have his own crew for moving his 16mm or 35mm camera, big lights, heavy production truck that gets eight or ten miles to the gallon, which you'll also be paying for, as well as feeding this circus and paying some portion of their normal day rate.

Once the shoot is over you'll still have the costs of negative cutting, mixing the audio and color timing, so factor in an additional $20,000 to $30,000 or even $50,000.

Your film will then be run in a rented screening room or independent theatre on a projector that could scratch your precious print on it's virgin screening. You will now have spent $50,000 to $100,000 for your 16mm or 35mm epic to screen in festivals (if you're accepted) and show to potential buyers for distribution.

In the end what will you have to show for all this? A $60,000 to $100,000 or $200,000 print for a film that will never see theatrical distribution. At best your baby may go out as a DVD, which costs less than a dollar to duplicate.

Oh! And your car, which you'll be living out of.

Bonnie Bennett with Mike Carroll during the early stages of editing *Dog Soldiers*, being cut tape-to-tape on a DVC Pro deck on the dining room table on weekends.

Have A Good Partner For The Journey

NOBODY WANTS TO GO THROUGH THIS ALONE. It's hard enough doing anything in life, particularly making a movie by yourself. Having a partner who is not on the same page with you can make it immeasurably difficult, if not impossible, to even consider. Luckily, that has not been the case for me. From the very outset of my independent filmmaking journey my wife Bonnie (mentioned throughout the book by her professional name Bonnie Bennett) has been encouraging me every step of the way.

After seeing *The Celebration* (*Festen*), which proved to the world that a great film could be shot on a consumer grade camcorder, I told Bonnie that I wanted to buy my own digital camcorder and start putting my filmmaking theories to the test. She responded, "I think you should. You need to do this." A few months later when I realized that the best way to edit the film would require getting a new computer and learning Final Cut Pro her reaction was, "Computers are where everything's heading. You need to start learning this now and get ahead of the pack."

A few years later I'd stepped up from the Sony TRV900 to the Sony PD150, inspired by what Michael Winterbottom had been able to achieve with the PAL version of the PD150 on *In This World*. The PD150 was about as perfect a DV camcorder as one could hope for, except for one thing: it only shot 30 frame video. George Lucas and Sony had just introduced the HDW-900F camera capable of a cinema-quality image and, most importantly, that could shoot video at 24 frames per second, the frame rate of motion picture film. DV filmmakers everywhere were aching to break away from the shackles of 30 frame video, which made our films look like videotaped soap operas. Within a year Panasonic introduced the DVX100 camcorder that shot video at 24 frames per second (24p) and *looked* like film.

This was about the time that I was getting close to shooting my first dramatic feature length film *Year*. I was very excited by this new development, but I was still a little dubious. Was camcorder 24p just a gimmick? After all, Michael Winterbottom's *In This World* had been shot on the Sony PD150 and looked amazing.

Then I learned that one of the news editors at the TV station where I work had just bought a Panasonic DVX100. One morning he brought his camera in and I brought my Sony PD150 and we did a test, walking around the station with our cameras rolling. I loaded both tapes into my MacBook, synched them up and arranged the shots so they were playing in side-by-side boxes. That evening I played the test footage out through a projector onto a big eight by eight foot screen.

Bonnie watched impressed. "Boy, your camera really looks good. Look at how rich that color is."

"Thanks, honey," I told her. "But that's the other guy's camera."

"Then you need to sell your camera and get one like his."

I posted my PD150 on eBay that night. It sold a few days later and I had a Panasonic DVX100A within a week.

Technology is always changing and you have to be ready to change with it. Having a partner in life and in art who is with you makes the trip so much sweeter.

My Personal Journey To Becoming A One-Man Filmmaker

I DIDN'T GO TO FILM SCHOOL. In fact, I bypassed college all together.

Right out of high school I got a job at a camera store. I'd seen Michelangelo Antonioni's *Blowup* and wanted a Nikon. I was determined to make my living with a camera. Whether still photography or cinematography, it's all cameras, lenses, composition and exposure.

Around this time there was an article in one of my hometown St. Louis newspapers about local TV news cameramen, back in the days when news was still being shot on 16mm film, which mentioned that most had started out in the mail room for a year or two, then transferred to the film processing lab in the news department. Immediately I thought that maybe a job shooting news with a movie camera, and getting paid for it, could be my portal into filmmaking.

I put on my nice clothes and made the rounds to all the local TV stations, filling out employment applications. One afternoon the following week I had nothing to do so I put my nice clothes back on, went back to the same TV stations and filled out the applications again. A few days later I did that again. This time the receptionists had clipboards with employment applications waiting for me as I came through the door. After the fourth or fifth visit one of the receptionists placed a call and got me an interview. A week later I was working in the mail room. My foot was in the door to my "on-the-job film school."

Starting in the mailroom was a great opportunity to get to know every department and the real day-to-day workings of a TV station, while getting paid at the same time. I got to know everybody and became good friends with a couple of the cameramen, including the cameraman-in-training who was running the film processing lab, whom I had replaced in the mail room.

In time I moved up into editing commercial breaks into movies and chopping them down to fit into the two-hour afternoon movie time slot. This meant taking a movie of any length and cutting it down to 97 minutes and 37 seconds with nine commercial breaks. I was once given Elia Kazan's *The Arrangement*, which runs 125 minutes, and had to cut out 28 minutes, which, I must say, made it better.

Up to this time video tape only existed in the engineering department in the form of huge two-inch wide reels. Then in the late-seventies came 3/4" video tape cassettes and portable recording decks and the age of E.N.G. (Electronic News Gathering) hit with a vengeance.

Almost overnight, TV news film cameramen across the country were out the door and engineers were given cameras and sent out to shoot news. Degrees in electronics and electrical engineering became a requirement. Knowledge of photography and filmmaking was deemed irrelevant. I was screwed.

Adrift as to what to do next, a cameraman friend gave me some pivotal career advice: "Trying to break into TV in a city this size is a tough nut to crack. Why don't you do what I did—get a job in a smaller market, get your experience and then you can go wherever you want."

One Saturday morning when the newsroom was empty I went into the tape library, pulled a couple of my friend's stories, put them on a tape and slapped my name on it. I made a bunch of copies and started mailing them out to every small market TV station in the Midwest that had an opening for a cameraman. Eventually I found a little station in Kansas with zero ratings where no cameraman with any experience wanted to work. Every week I'd get a call from the news director saying, "I have an opening for a photographer, but you don't have a lot of experience." The next week he'd call me back and say, "I appreciate your interest, but I offered the job to a guy who's been shooting for two years up in Des Moines. You want me to send your tape back?"

"No, no, you keep it. I like what I hear about your place and I'd like you to keep me in mind if anything else comes up."

The following week he called me back, "The guy's wife doesn't want to leave Iowa. You still interested?"

"You bet I am."

"All right, I'll get back to you."

The next week, "I like your desire, Mike, but I've got a guy in Nebraska who's been working in a bureau and I offered him the job."

"All right, I understand. But if he changes his mind, I'm still here."

"I like your willingness. I'll get back to you."

A few days passed and I hadn't heard anything so I called him back. "Mike, I was just going to call you. The bastard turned me down so, what the hell, come on out to Wichita."

That's how I became a cameraman—because no one else would take the job.

That was a Wednesday morning. By noon I'd given my notice. Not two weeks, but two days. I wanted to get out to Kansas before they could change their mind. That Friday, after leaving my first TV job, my then-wife and I packed into the car and headed 400 miles west on I-70 to our new home somewhere in Kansas. I didn't know where the place was or how to spell its name. I had to call a hotel there and ask the desk clerk, "I'm driving from St. Louis, Missouri. How do I get to Wichita?"

Saturday was spent apartment hunting, but that night I paid a visit to the station situated on the outskirts of town. I was given a tour, then settled into an editing room where one of the shooters was cutting a story. His name was Ray and he gave me the lowdown on how they did things. "We don't do any pans or zooms here. Everything's static. We let all our action go in and out of frame, and no jump cuts." I had no idea what he was talking about.

I asked Ray about the cameras they used.

"Oh, yeah. We use Sharps. They're cheap industrial cameras. You're from St. Louis, you're probably used to Ikegamis. These are a little different." He put a Sharp up on a desk and pointed out all the buttons and controls, then he left to go to the bathroom. The second he was out the door I scrambled for a sheet of paper and scribbled down everything he'd just said. I think he could tell from how I was looking over the camera and watching him edit that I didn't know anything.

When I officially started work I taped a 3x5 card to the side of my Sharp with typed instructions starting with: "1) Turn camera ON. 2) White balance." And so on.

I hit the ground running. Shooting, recording sound, editing on deadline. Trial by fire. Every day I thought I'd be found out and fired. Every day my coworkers were trying to get me fired. The one thing that saved me was that when I was given an assignment I grabbed it and headed out the door. This was defensive strategy -- out of sight and out of mind. My boss saw it as enthusiasm and kept me on. I also learned that in TV news no matter how bad your shooting is, the most important thing is bringing something back and getting it on air.

During the first week I left everything on automatic and just concentrated on not bringing back green or blue video. It also became clear that I couldn't become a good news photographer overnight, so I started my own self-education strategy: every week I was going to take one aspect of the job and get better at it.

FIRST WEEK: Just get through it & learn how the gear works
SECOND WEEK: Shoot handheld & make shots steady
THIRD WEEK: Record audio on manual settings
FOURTH WEEK: Concentrate on shooting in sequences – long shot to establish, medium shot on the subjects, close-ups on the action
FIFTH WEEK: Shoot everything on tripod
SIXTH WEEK: Improve lighting for interviews
ALWAYS: Pick up editing speed

Instead of getting overwhelmed with trying to fix my shortcomings all at once, I worked on them incrementally, one step at a time. Using this systematic approach, within a couple months I transformed myself into a much more competent and reliable shooter, and every week I got a little better than I was before.

If I was given a story that would take an hour to cut, I'd force myself to cut it in forty-five minutes, then thirty minutes or less to get comfortable with editing under pressure.

This was my film school and my indoctrination to becoming a professional. The great thing about this film school was that I was shooting every day and every evening it would be on-the-air, broadcast to hundreds of thousands of people across the state. I could watch the story I'd shot in the newsroom on the row of monitors and see how the shooters for the other stations shot the same story and compare different ways of seeing the same scene. And I was getting paid for it.

For a quarter of a century now I've been a professional cameraman shooting TV news and documentaries. Five days a week I have a camera on my shoulder and at the end of the day I cut my footage for broadcasting. Experience has trained me to be able to walk into almost any situation and be ready to start shooting.

On assignment in the high Sierras. TV news as film school. Learning under fire.

In the days of the great studios everyone on the lot was a staff or contract employee. Monday through Friday, 8 to 5, they made movies. If a film wrapped on Wednesday, they'd have a new assignment on Thursday. Five days a week they did their job, practicing their craft, trying new things. Comedies, tragedies, action-adventures, character dramas. They'd shoot on sound stages, back lots and real locations.

You don't become a pro by accident. It's the result of steady, concentrated work. Nowadays you can buy a professional-quality HD camcorder for just a couple thousand bucks. If you have a film you want to make but your script's not ready yet, don't wait—pick up an inexpensive digital camcorder and start developing your eye. Film your yard, the leaves on the trees, the angle of the light at different times of day. Film your family to learn how to follow action. When playing back your footage look at it objectively. Compare your shots to ones you've seen in movies. Learn to distinguish what makes a shot good and what doesn't. Keep an eye out for distracting telephone lines in the background and phone poles spiking up out of people's heads.

> The more you shoot, the better you get. This goes for writing, acting, editing—anything. The sooner you start, the quicker you'll get there.

Year—Test Out Concepts With Test Footage

WHEN I GET AN IDEA FOR A FILM I START SHOOTING TEST FOOTAGE early on to see how it's going to work. When I was writing *Year* I knew that I wanted to punctuate sequences with music and time-lapse shots. It would be unique, beautiful to watch and, hopefully, help the film to stand out visually.

I'd been enormously taken by a time-lapse sequence in Michael Winterbottom's *Wonderland* of a young woman walking down London sidewalks at night. This got me to thinking about interweaving time-lapse footage into regular storytelling.

Whenever I'd see some interesting clouds rolling overhead I'd set up a camcorder on a tripod in the backyard and let it roll for fifteen minutes to an hour. Clouds by themselves in real-time can be beautiful, but sped up ten or twenty or fifty times, accompanied by some interesting music, and they become magical. Within a couple months I had twenty hours of footage loaded into Final Cut Pro and compressed to thirty minutes of time-lapse material.

I wanted the soundtrack for *Year* to be new-age electronic music. "Mind music," I called it. I turned to a friend and coworker, Tom DuHain, who is a new-age music aficionado.

Right away Tom said, "You know, I was just listening to something that sounded very interesting." He punched up the website of an independent label called Spotted Peccary Music (spottedpeccary.com) and started playing a sample.

After hearing ten seconds I said, "That's the sound!"

The music was *Wind Journey*, a CD by Norwegian musician Erik Wollø, which had already been out for two years. I ordered the CD that night.

When it arrived I loaded it into my computer and laid it under the time-lapse footage. As Bonnie and I started meeting with actors we were considering for the movie I'd run this tape for them and very soon their eyes would go wide at the beauty of the clouds and the music. This helped them to get a glimpse of the movie I had in mind, made them feel comfortable with me and got them excited about being a part of the project.

Take Your Filmmaking Seriously

While making *Year* an Emmy-winning producer friend once asked how the film was coming. I was a bit reluctant to say much as my entire movie was being made for less than the catering budget of one his projects.

"Look, I know that I probably sound like somebody making another little camcorder movie to you, but I just feel that if I don't take it seriously and treat it like a real film then what's the point."

"That's exactly right," he responded. "That's the only way you can do it. How much a movie costs isn't important. What matters is having the passion to make something good."

> **Good filmmaking gets down to one person with passion who stays with it.**

Financing? Or Scamming?

ONE DAY I WAS IN AN ARTS HIGH SCHOOL shooting a story for my TV news day job and the reporter I was working with mentioned that I made independent films.

"Oh, really?" the woman who ran the school perked up. "Shorts or music videos?"

"Features."

"Features? You mean a whole movie?"

"Yeah."

"So you direct them?"

"Yeah."

"Who produces them?"

"My wife and I do."

"Where do you get your financing?"

"My wife and I pay for them."

"Where do you find your writers?"

"I write them."

"What about your crews? Who shoots them?"

"I do."

"Who does the sound?"

"I do."

"Who edits them?"

"I do."

"So you do everything?"

"I have to. Nobody's gonna do it for me."

I make my movies with my own money. It's not because I'm rich, because I'm not. I'm just a regular guy who works for a living. I made *Dog Soldiers* to see how well the new digital camcorders worked and to see if I could make a long-form documentary. With the next film, *Year*, I wanted to apply what I'd learned to making a feature-length dramatic film, from a script, with actors, to see if one-man filmmaking could work. With *Nightbeats* I needed to prove that it wasn't a fluke and that I could do it again, and better.

Each of these projects were experiments to see if the filmmaking theories that I'd been espousing (and boring people with) over the years could really be done. I could never have attempted this with somebody else's hard-earned money. If I'd taken investors and the films hadn't worked out, what would I say? "Thanks for putting your faith and confidence in me. Sorry the films were a failure. I gave it my best shot. Had a lotta fun. Learned a lot. The next one's gonna be better. How much dough you got left?"

I know people who make music videos and five and ten minute short films as their stepping-stones toward making features. They have scripts in their pockets and talk about raising $300,000 or $500,000 or a million to finance their movie so they can pay everyone the industry standard. Including paying themselves the Writers Guild, Producers Guild and Directors Guild minimum fees of $30,000-$50,000, allowing them to rake in over $100,000 before shooting a frame.

Investment plans like that always make me wonder how many times they've seen *The Producers*. Why would anybody invest their savings in complete unknowns? You make a nice music video, fine. But entertaining an audience for three minutes is nothing compared to keeping them involved for 80 to 100 minutes. If I were to help out a first-time feature filmmaker with some of my own hard-earned bread I'd want to see every penny up on the screen—and *not* going toward paying their rent.

Before a first-time filmmaker tries to reach out to an investor they need to first reach into their own pockets and credit cards and make a full-length movie to prove that they can tell a story for an hour and a half. Show me you can do that, and do it well, and then you've earned the right to ask others to risk their money on you.

You Can Still Be Orson Welles

EVERY YOUNG FILMMAKER WANTS TO BE ORSON WELLEs and make their own *Citizen Kane* by the time they're 24. I know I did. If you're not yet 24, there's still time. If 24's behind you then you can still be Orson Welles. Not the Orson Welles of the RKO years but the Orson Welles of his later years when he made his films with his own money and his own camera (a French Eclair Cameflex), edited on his own editing machine in his own house. And just like the independent Orson Welles, you too will have to struggle to get your films seen.

Make An Impact On Your Audience

ONE OF THE GREATEST REWARDS FROM HAVING MADE *YEAR* was the experience of people coming up to me days or weeks after they'd seen it to say, "You know, I can't stop thinking about the women in your movie. What happens to the girl having the baby? And the singer, is she going back on the stage? What happens next to all those people?" I made it a rule to always reply, "What do you think happens to them?" It's fascinating to hear the stories that other people weave for the characters that I made up and everybody's take is a little bit different, which was exactly what I wanted. My goal with *Year* was to connect with audiences on an emotional level and get the wheels of their minds turning so that after the movie was over the characters would continue to live on in their imagination.

CAMERAS & Getting Started

First camcorder: Sony TRV900 camera, BeachTek audio adapter mounted to the bottom, Sennheiser headphones.

Your Camera—Learn It Inside & Out

I STARTED RIDING THE DIGITAL WAVE IN 1999 with my first camcorder, the Sony TRV900. Quite a high-end camcorder for its time. It had three chips producing a sharp 500 scan line image, almost the equivalent of broadcast television, and a stereo microphone input for plugging in an external XLR adapter to use professional wireless and shotgun mics.

I bought the camera ($2,250 at the time) to jump into the emerging digital revolution with a documentary, *Dog Soldiers*, about professional dog walkers in New York City. UPS delivered the camera just a few weeks before Bonnie and I left for New York to see her daughter Lori and the grandson Sam and for me to shoot the film.

Fresh out of the box, I turned the TRV900 on, flipped out the LCD screen and, without having to set up a thing, it looked great. The automatic white balance, auto-focus, automatic audio recording—everything about the camera (not to mention weighing only 1.5 pounds) took all the work out of shooting. In fact, I did all the shooting in New York on auto-white balance only to discover later that there were manual controls.

Get To Know Your Camera.

Don't just show up and start shooting. You can't be pulling out the owner's manual while filming.

Shoot simple things around the house and neighborhood to test how the camera handles:

- low light
- bright light
- autofocus accuracy
- auto iris response
- ease of manual iris

Three things to do with a new piece of gear:

> **Test it**
> **Test it again**
> **Test it a third time to confirm the first two tests**

Built-In Mics

Some camcorders come with the built-in mic on the top. This is completely worthless. Your camcorder's lens is filming what is in front of you so you don't need a mic that records sound happening directly above you. Get a camcorder with the in-board microphone in front and below the lens because sound comes *at* you.

If you're planning on using the built-in mic[1] you've got to try it out in all kinds of different situations to know its strengths and weaknesses:

> People talking indoors and outdoors
> General action—how it picks up ambient or natural sound
> How it works in wind
> Whether it picks up any sound from your hands holding the camera
> How close you have to get the camera in order to hear someone or something the clearest
> How much of the tinny background room sound it picks up

SOUND ADVICE: When shooting a documentary, much of your footage will be grabbed on the run. You're not going to have time to put a wireless mic on everybody. Make sure you've got a good built-in or externally attached mic that's up to the job.

Some Built-In Mics Can Be Incredibly Good

The Sony TRV900 camcorder had built-in stereo mics in front below the lens with a side stereo input for plugging in external audio mics. I'd always shot news with an external Sennheiser shotgun mic and was skeptical of built-in mics. Impressively, the Sony built-in mics seemed to have built-in radar that automatically responded to the sound nearest the camera and dampened other sounds in the background.

This wound up being enormously helpful for grabbing interviews with people on the street. One time I was in a park along the East River when a group of walkers came up and took a break to give their dogs water. I slowly worked my way up, filming their interactivity with the dogs. As I approached the lead walker, a charming young man from South America named Paulo, was very easygoing and happy to talk about the dogs and his technique. I didn't want to risk intimidating him by pulling out the wireless microphone so I just held the camera off to the side and kept rolling as he talked.

---

1 This goes for both the camcorders that have the microphones built into the camera body and the higher-end prosumer camcorders that come with small external shotgun mics.

It was a gamble shooting the interview this way but I was afraid that I'd scare him off if I looked too professional, which is also why I didn't pull out my headphones. Sometimes it's better to take a chance on shooting something that's not going to come out rather than not get the footage at all. To further complicate the situation, there was major construction going on a few blocks away filling the area with the rumble of heavy machinery. However, when I checked the footage later Paulo's interview came out perfectly and the construction sound was only barely noticeable. From that moment on I became a big fan of Sony's built-in mics.

> SOUND ADVICE: When using a built-in mic to record the primary audio, the closer you get to your subject the cleaner the audio.

> MANUFACTURER'S WARNING: Every brand is different. Sony, Canon, JVC, Samsung, etc. Just because you're familiar with the sound you get out of one brand's camera, don't expect it to be the same on another name brand.

> SOUND ADVICE: Controlling your audio levels manually will result in cleaner sound.

Wide Angle For Documentary

I find that wide angle works best for documentaries and telephoto works best for dramatic or comedic material. With dramatic films, if you miss something you can always shoot another take. On a documentary your action happens one time and that's it. A wide-angle lens will help keep everything in the frame[2]. A good lens for that is a .5 wide angle attachment, which is 50% wider than your camcorder's lens at its widest, allowing you to:

> Get in closer to the action
> Get a visually dynamic perspective that is exciting to the eye

Using a wide-angle lens on autofocus you can get a lot of terrific off-the-cuff footage without ever looking through the lens or flip-out screen. The goal of documentary shooting is to be invisible. Using a wide-angle lens attachment and not always looking at the flip-out screen can get you close to that.

---

2 This is not a hard and fast rule, just something useful when starting out. The more you shoot and the more films you make the more comfortable you'll be with shooting documentary in telephoto. Certainly for shooting wildlife and nature filmmaking you'd be dead without a super-telephoto and a sturdy tripod. But starting out documenting your family and/or friends to get some practice you'll find a wide-angle lens to be one of your best friends.

Gear: Buy The Best—Be The Best

WHEN I'M SHOOTING THERE'S SO MUCH ON MY MIND that the last thing I want to deal with is faulty equipment so I always go with reliable names—Sony, Canon, Panasonic, JVC, Sennheiser, Sachtler. Big names with reputations for good products and service.

Buying cheap only comes back to bite you later. For example, a $200 shotgun microphone versus a Sennheiser for $500 or $600. The $200 shotgun may sound fine when you're shooting, but if there's the slightest background hiss when it's played back over high-end speakers that's the way your whole film will sound.

I started out as a cameraman at a small TV station where the tripods were old and battered so we shot off the shoulder most of the time. But if I was going to make my footage look better, which would improve my resume tape and lead to a higher-paying job in a bigger city, I needed to invest in myself.

I went to the bank, took out an equity loan against my car and spent $3,500 on my own Sachtler tripod, the same tripod the network news crews used. This was in 1987 when the tripod that I'd been issued cost around $800 and I was making all of $17,000 a year. (That same Sachtler tripod in 2009 would run about $12,000.) Having made that investment I was committed to shooting everything I could on the Sachtler.

Instantly, my footage started to stand out. It was now effortless to make smooth pans and tilts. With a few minor adjustments I could raise and lower the legs in seconds. I rarely shot anything "off the sticks." Within a year my photography had won a dozen statewide and regional awards. A year after that I had over thirty awards on my resume and landed a job in Sacramento, California, at the NBC-affiliate, earning significantly more.

At the new station cameramen were issued Sachtler tripods as part of their regular gear, so I advertised my Sachtler in nearby San Francisco and sold it for $1,800.

Rent Gear To Check It Out

If there's a specific camera I'm considering for a film I'll try to rent it to test out first. Trying out a camera for a couple hundred dollars over a weekend could save an awful lot of headache later.

If you contact a company that both rents and sells, and there are several in L.A., let them know you're in the market for a camera and what you're looking to use it on. They may offer a weekend rental deal: you rent the camera you're interested in, they ship it to you and if you decide after testing that you want to buy it they will very likely be glad to deduct the rental from the purchase price.

Changing Cameras—Changing Formats

Filming *Nightbeats* with the JVC GY HD110U HDV camcorder. As soon as the shoot was completed the camera was sold to a fellow filmmaker who has gone on to shoot a series of award-winning zombie horror films.

Dog Soldiers, Year and *Nightbeats* were all shot with different cameras that recorded to mini-DV tapes. As technology has changed so have I. Tapeless is the current rule of the day and I'm going with it. Friends of mine who've worked with the RED camera tell me that they can never go back. I've just invested (at this writing in March 2010) in the Canon 7D DSLR that shoots high-quality stills and full resolution 1080 HD in 24p. There are tradeoffs, but you adapt and overcome.

I have a cinematographer friend who has 35mm film in his veins and says, "This whole digital thing is a craze, but you can't beat film. Just wait, it's coming back." He says that. *He really says that!* But until the "digital craze" passes even he's shooting with the RED.

There's Always Another Camera

I hang on to my equipment until I've finished shooting and am far enough into the editing to I know that I've got everything I need, then I post the camera in a local filmmakers newsletter or on eBay.

I'm a camera junkie. I love working with the best, latest toy out there. But cameras and computers change so rapidly that I've created a filmmaker's rule:

> Buy the latest technology camera for each new project.
> Sell the camera as soon as the project's over.

A Camera Is Not A Wife, But A Lover

Use it, then cast it aside when something better comes along. Change your e-mail, don't return calls and never look back.

The Great eBay Clearing House

For many people, making a movie is just another goal on the checklist of life, along with climbing Everest and trying out for American Idol. Get it out of the system and move on. Others simply assume they're naturally imbued with the golden DNA that guarantees a smash at Sundance and the red carpet walk on *ET Hollywood*. The truth is very few films ever make it into legitimate out-of-town festivals where a film is selected solely on its merit.

"Man, I didn't realize it was going to be so much work."

Few people have the perseverance to stay with D.I.Y. moviemaking for more than a few years. One or two movies and they're out. They post their gear on Craigslist and eBay to recoup some of their cash and provide great deals for the next wave of filmmakers coming in, meaning you.

Through eBay I got an incredible Sennheiser pistol grip and mic zeppelin worth $700-$800 retail for only $300 and a classic 35mm Moviola editing machine that was once part of the Universal Studios editing department, originally valued at over $10,000, for a mere $250.

My Head-Up-My-Ass Moment

A COUPLE YEARS AGO I WAS DRIVING TO A NEWS STORY and the reporter I was working with asked me how *Year* was coming, then asked what kind of shows I watched. I told her I didn't have time to watch TV, that all my time was spent in front of the Emac editing my movie.

Then I started to go off.

"Why should I waste my time watching other people's stuff? Why should any of us? With the new digital technology we should be out making our own shows. Why should we watch anything when we can turn on our camcorders and make our own programming?" (This was before Youtube.)

During this the reporter sat quietly looking out the window, but I could tell by her little smile that she was thinking, "Has this guy got his head up his ass." It's easy when you're deep into making a film to lose sight of the forest for the trees and that's all you can think of or talk about. As a result people stop talking to you lest they have to suffer the latest installment of your cinematic saga.

I now make it a policy to never discuss my movies unless directly asked and then to keep my response brief. "Same old, same old. I'm a broken record." Instead, I post updates to a blog on my website. People can read them or not. The next day I'll usually hear comments like, "Hey, sounds like it's really coming along," or "Cool stuff on the website. Can't wait to see it." I leave it at that and find that most people still talk to me this way.

Get Your Feet Wet: Make A Film About The People Around You

I CAN'T JUST WANDER AROUND FILMING RANDOM STUFF. I need a purpose. Before we set off for New York to shoot the dog walkers documentary I needed to run the Sony TRV900 camera through the ropes to see how professionally I could make the footage look and sound.

I love the relationship my wife Bonnie has with her oldest daughter Lori, so I decided to make a little documentary about the two of them. They're very similar people. Strong, talented. Almost mirror images in many ways. And genuine friends with an extraordinary bond that goes beyond the typical mother-daughter dynamic.

If you're thinking about making a film, don't wait until you start doing your project. Start shooting early on to familiarize yourself with the camera and find out:

Frames from *The Ultimate Home Movie*. Bonnie on the phone to daughter Lori. Lori and then-2 year old Sam.

What you can do with a camera
How people react to you with a camera
How you see things compositionally
Where you need to improve
How your footage edits together

All my professional experience to that point had been in TV news, telling stories in a minute and a half, which I saw as mini-moviemaking. With this experimental documentary, using a radically smaller camera, I wanted to explore free form shooting and editing styles and test out long form storytelling. This exercise eventually became a 45 minute film called *Bonnie, Lori & Sam: The Ultimate*

Home Movie that tested every feature the TRV900 had to offer, going from color to black & white to sepia and alternating between full-frame 4:3 to letterbox, all in-camera effects.

This may sound extremely basic, making a documentary about your family as a test project, and you may get some flack while you're doing it. However, you'll find that as the years roll on your elaborate home movie will become increasingly cherished by the people in it as a document of a specific moment in their lives.

Camcorder Photojournalism In Action

During the lead-up to the 2008 Beijing Olympics I was on assignment at United Nations Plaza in San Francisco where Buddhist monks were announcing their plans to peacefully disrupt the Olympic torch run to bring attention to civil rights abuses in Tibet. It was a packed crowd and I was struggling to get any kind of a shot with my whale-sized 30 pound Ikegami news camera while internet activists with camcorders were running rings around me with camcorders and immediately uploading their footage to the internet.

When shooting in crowds there's no better tool than a camcorder. I used my Sony TRV900 the same way years earlier at Embarcadero Square on December 31, 1999, covering the changeover to the new millennium. It was a huge event with thousands of partying San Franciscans. Cameramen from other stations were moving through the crowd with bulky BetaCams on their shoulders shooting the heads of all the people crushed in around them, while I simply raised the TRV900 up over my head and got a perfectly clear shot when the clock struck midnight, the fireworks went off and the crowd burst into celebration. I swooped my camcorder down on people cheering, popping champagne, kissing. I saved the footage and used it as "live" news coverage in *Year*.

A major hindrance when filming with a big news camera is that your field of vision is cut in half by the camera on your shoulder, blocking your view of anything happening off to your right. With a camcorder you're free to see everything.

You can get a camcorder into places that aren't possible with a big camera and you have more energy because there's no weight to wear you down.

One of the biggest bonuses to shooting with a camcorder is that nobody takes you seriously. You can shoot almost anything anywhere and, as long as you look and act like an innocent tourist, chances are pretty good you won't be bothered.

Making It Big On MTV—Little Camera, Big Results

ONE OF THE REPORTERS I WORKED WITH, Gina Garcia, had profiled the Sacramento-based band Cake for a news story and wound up marrying the band's trumpet player, Vince Di Fiore. Around that time Gina came to the Sacramento Film Festival screening of *Dog Soldiers*, saw that I could shoot more than news and encouraged her husband to bring me aboard for their next music video.

For *Short Skirt, Long Jacket* the band's leader John McCrea was the producer-director. Three separate crews were used: one in San Francisco, one at Venice Beach in Los Angeles, and one here in Sacramento. The Venice Beach and San Francisco crews were both two-person crews of cameraman and soundman who divided a one-day rate of $600. I told John that I could work faster doing both jobs myself. John didn't care as long as I delivered the footage, so I one-manned it and pocketed the whole $600.

The concept for the video was a bit radical. As John explained it to me, the two other crews wandered around randomly asking people to listen to a new song and then were filmed as they said whatever came into their heads about the music, lyrics, beat, style, whatever.

The soundman would give the person a pair of headphones and the cameraman would frame up on a CD player as the soundman hit "Play," giving John a synch point to match up the music. Then the cameraman would whip the camera over to the person's face for their reactions until the song was over.

(NOTE: This next part is technical.)

This seemed like a Rube Goldberg device to me. In the place of a soundman I bought a $2 Y-cable at Radio Shack, plugged it into the CD player, plugged the headphone jack into one end of the Y-cable while the other end of the Y-cable fed into an input on the BeachTek adapter feeding into the Sony TRV900. This allowed Cake's song to be fed directly into the Sony camcorder's Audio One channel. To record people's comments about the song I used a Sony ECM 55 lavalier microphone connected to the BeachTek's second audio input feeding into the Sony camcorder's Audio Two channel. This way everything was synched up on the tape and John didn't have to synch it up later in editing.

Editing with John McKrea and Vince Di Fiore of *Cake*.

The video for *Short Skirt, Long Jacket* was unusual in that you never saw the band at all. Instead, the video shows these random people on the streets of San Francisco, Venice Beach and Sacramento listening to the song and talking over it. And anybody who *didn't* like the song was certain to be featured prominently.

The record company hated it. They didn't like the low-end camcorder production value, didn't like people talking over the music, and absolutely detested seeing people saying they didn't like the song. One lone forward-thinking young executive felt it was out-of-the-box enough that MTV might go for it. *Short Skirt, Long Jacket* went on to become the eighth most requested video on MTV that summer.

I was crossing the newsroom a few months later when a fellow cameraman called out, "Hey, congrats on the nomination."

I didn't know what he meant. I hadn't entered any TV news contests in years. "No, the MTV award." Unbeknownst to me *Short Skirt, Long Jacket* had been nominated for Breakthrough Music Video in the MTV Awards.

The award wound up going to a big name band for a high-budget computer-animated video. If we had won, the award would have gone to Cake and John McCrea as director. But when somebody congratulates you on being associated with a major award, milk it, baby, milk it.

A Crew (Nightmare) Story

CAKE MUST'VE THOUGHT I WAS GOOD LUCK FOR THEM because they took me along as part of the crew when the record company demanded that their next video, *Love You Madly*, be shot in Los Angeles.

A music industry financial note about music videos: bands are responsible for half the production costs of music videos, which is deducted from the sales revenue of their music, and can be a significant chunk of their income.

"Okay, you've done your no-budget experimental video," Cake's record company told them. "Now you have to make a real one." This meant shooting in L.A. and contracting with an L.A. production company. They attached me to the project at the day rate they'd established, which was better than what any of the L.A. crew was making, because they wanted to have a familiar face on the set.

The production company recommended using digital BetaCams for the shoot. Of course, they would. BetaCams were high-ticket items and production companies get a percentage commission based on how much is spent on a shoot, so the more expensive the gear the higher their commission. Cake's band leader John McCrea, who was again directing, called for my input and I urged him to consider the Canon XL-1 mini-DV camcorder. There would be little noticeable difference in picture quality, plus Sony BetaCams rented for $600-$800 a day whereas an XL-1 went for $175 or less.

The concept for the video was to be a documentary of a gourmet cooking contest as trumpeter Vince Di Fiore and drummer Pete McNeal cooked their favorite dishes for a panel of celebrity judges.

I flew into LAX and took a cab to the location at a cooking academy in Santa Monica. As I got close I saw trucks, trailers, crew, gear belts, tape measures, rolls of gaffers tape in every imaginable color. My first thought was that there was a movie shooting in the same area as our music video. Then the cab let me out right in the middle of this circus. Suddenly it became clear that this was all for the "real one" the record company had demanded.

I found the D.P. (Director of Photography) bolting an XL-1 onto a pan head on a camera dolly. The XL-1 has a curve on the bottom so it had some wiggle room on the flat-topped pan head. The D.P. was about to send one of his assistants back to the rental house[3] to rent some widget to make the camera more stable. That's when I introduced myself as one of his camera operators for the day, then tore a couple narrow strips from a roll of gaffer's tape and layered them onto the bottom of the XL-1 to create some cushioning, bolted the camera back onto the pan head and *voila*, it was rock solid. The D.P. shook his head with mild amusement at this solution.

The crew apparently worked together frequently because they all knew each other well and gave me only passing mind. A short while later a limousine pulled up and John McCrea, Vince Di Fiore and Pete McCrea poured out. People from the production company and the D.P. and 1st A.D. all lined up to greet them but the band just went right past them and up to me, shaking my hand and saying how glad they were to have me with them on this one. Then they turned to meet the D.P. and the 1st A.D. and the rest of the crew whom they were forced to hire.

The setup seemed to take hours while a couple gaffers tried to figure out where to place some Kino Flo lights. The D.P. scratched his chin, pointing out one place and then another, but was essentially indifferent.

It wasn't my place to interfere but finally I suggested, "Why don't you just set them up here and here to fill in the existing overhead lighting?"

"Yeah, that sounds pretty good," the D.P. said and turned away. He had quite a few major videos under his belt, but on this shoot he spent most of the day seated on the camera dolly. I think that since we were shooting mini-DV and not Betacam or 16mm or 35mm he couldn't have cared less.

Five minutes later we were ready to go. The 1st A.D. put on a wireless headset. He was also the only member of the crew wearing a headset. Just who he was talking to neither director John McCrea or I had any idea or ever found out. The 1st A.D. then called out, "Okay, people. Quiet on the set. We're going to get rolling here. Let's go to one." Before he could get another word out John was pointing out for the cameras to go here and there and we were rolling. All the 1st A.D. could do was stand out of the way and watch.

This was essentially a docu shoot so I was in my element. John pretty much left me alone to do my thing and spent most of his time with the other camera operator, who didn't seem that familiar with shooting on-the-fly but quickly caught on. During this I don't think the D.P. ever left

[3] Hollywood crews feel the solution to every problem requires a highly specialized and overpriced gadget from a rental house.

his place on the camera dolly. He'd occasionally squint through the XL-1 and roll on something, but a good 90% of the shoot was accomplished by just John, the other handheld cameraman and myself. The rest of the crew was getting paid basically to just be there.

On top of that, two separate caterers had been hired to feed this army. A lunch caterer was set up on a parking lot a block away with a tent, tables, chairs and security guards to protect it all, as well as an on-set caterer with an elaborate craft services table piled high with croissants, lunch meats, cheese, cookies, fresh fruit, nuts, etc. Every thirty minutes she'd parade through the set with trays of iced coffees, fruit yogurts, hors d'oeuvres and sushi, to which the 1st A.D. and the D.P. and the otherwise idle crew would swarm like starving flies. Meanwhile, Vince Di Fiore, drummer Pete McNeal, director John McCrea, the other cameraman and I kept filming.

As if the crew wasn't gorged enough on the bounty of the craft services table and the regular stream of treats being brought to them on trays, an hour or so into the shoot the 1st A.D. called "Lunch," and the crew that was doing nothing vanished like Houdini. John wanted to keep going and asked "Mike, do you mind sticking around with me and getting some more shooting done before you take a break?" Without hesitating I said, "Yeah, sure, you bet." We kept shooting through lunch, then John cut me loose to grab a quick bite, then get back to the set.

The video culminates when the dishes Vince and Pete made are judged by a celebrity panel made up of musician Rick James, comedian Phyllis Diller and chef Jeff Smith of "The Frugal Gourmet." The sound for this was done by a strapping, well-dressed fellow wielding a spotless new carbon fiber boom pole with a microphone zeppelin covered by a beautiful new windscreen furry that he'd taken out of the plastic bag only moments before. Right off the bat I knew something about this was not right. For one thing, there's no reason to have a furry wind cover on a microphone when you're recording sound inside. Secondly, he wasn't wearing headphones. If he had been wearing headphones he would have known that his heavily wind-protected microphone was not turned on. All of his beautiful and impressive-looking new gear wasn't recording a single decibel of anything the celebrity judges said.

Fortunately there was a cameraman shooting behind-the-scenes material and John managed to synch sound from his footage to salvage the video in the editing room.

Later that evening on the flight back from L.A. John McCrea sat next to me and unloaded about all the costs and battles he'd had with the record company and the production company leading up to the day's shoot. It had been a bitter experience that he vowed never to suffer or be forced to pay for again.

WRITING: A Script You Can Make

CARRE HOUSE   NIGHT

IDE SHOT: THE ROOM with everyone.

EVERYONE
Happy New Year!

ıts, laughter, hugs, kisses.   Chamı

Ava and Brendan - New Year's kissı
en go separate ways.

- Sydney fleetingly kisses Miles.

-- Ava gives Lana a hug.   Some loc
after their exchange earlier.

-- Gina and Chris kiss.

-- John Cassavetes moves to giv
so his lips just miss hers and
- she turns, giving her fri
- of place.   - share a

Where It All Starts—The Page

"Writing a screenplay is a very practical thing."
Sir David Lean, director *Lawrence of Arabia*

AFTER WORLD WAR II THE HOT THING WAS TO WRITE THE GREAT AMERICAN NOVEL. For the past 20 years it's changed to how to cash in on the Great American Screenplay.

The worst thing that ever happened to screenwriting was the day *Variety* reported that Joe Eszterhas had sold his spec script *Basic Instinct* for $3.5 million. Ever since then how-to screenwriting books have become bestsellers and workshops have become big draws packed with people wanting a fast track to wealth, fame and early retirement.

These are people who'd never even consider attempting a novel because that would require having to pound out four or five hundred pages and could require a year or more of work. Even worse than that, it would require actually being able to write. Whereas a screenplay only has to be a hundred pages and most of a screenplay is dialogue, and if you can talk you should be able to write dialogue. Plus, with screenwriting software that makes the writing even easier, this should be like taking money from a baby. Or is it candy from a baby? Whatever, just take it.

> FIRST RULE TO NEW SCREENWRITERS: The first script you write is usually loaded with every idea you've ever had -- flat jokes, reactions to one-liners, far too many speaking parts and runs around 200 pages long. I know my first one was. Write a few scripts to get the "bad writing" out of your system.

Read Before You Write

When people first start thinking about writing a screenplay they usually start by reading one of the how-to-write-a-screenplay books by Syd Field or Lew Hunter. Both are great teachers who'll provide you with a solid foundation of what a script is, plot, character, formats, etc. The essentials all laid out in plain language. I should mention that Lew judged a screenwriting contest a few years ago, which I'm pleased to say I won, and he's always been on the other end of the phone or an e-mail whenever I've had a question.

Before you can start writing a screenplay, though, you've got to know what good screenwriting is. The way to do that is to read screenplays. Fortunately, that's easy these days. Hundreds of screenplays have been published. Unfortunately, most of those have been revised to resemble the finished films. Personally, I prefer seeing what the screenplay looked like before they started making it. You can find quite a number of production scripts used on films and TV shows on eBay. There are also several websites where you can download scripts for free. You can also purchase scripts online from Script City (scriptcity.com) and either have photocopies sent to you or PDFs e-mailed.

Some of the best written scripts I've read are:

21 Grams	Guillermo Arriaga
Clean And Sober	Todd Carroll
	& Glenn Gordon Caron
The Godfather I & II	Francis Ford Coppola
Julia	Alvin Sargent
Kramer Vs. Kramer	Robert Benton
The Law	Joel Oliansky
Light Sleeper	Paul Schrader
Michael Clayton	Tony Gilroy
Monster's Ball	Milo Addica
	& Will Rokos
The Paper Chase	James Bridges
Places In The Heart	Robert Benton
Talk To Her	Pedro Almadovar
A Very British Coup	Alan Plater

Move to L.A. Or Make It Yourself

If you're an aspiring screenwriter living in St. Louis, Sacramento, Boise, Akron, Cleveland, Des Moines, Springfield or anywhere else outside of Los Angeles, and you don't plan on making the move to L.A., then unless you win a Nicholl Screenwriting Fellowship or some other high-profile writing competition no one is going to bother with you or your script. The reason is very simple: movies are made in L.A. You either go where the work is or you don't work.

Hollywood can be a closed shop unless you're an alumnus of the USC or UCLA film schools and are able to buddy up to one of the rising stars and schmooze a gig as staff writer on a series.

I started writing as a teenager, then for a long time had writer's block and couldn't finish anything. To jump-start myself I took a screenwriting course where I had to crank out pages on a deadline and my work would be scrutinized.

The first assignment was to write a 10-page treatment of our story idea. I've never quite understood treatments so I hammered out the whole script in an 85-page "scriptment" (more on "scriptments" later).

All of a sudden I felt like I had a full tank of high-octane and was ready to blast out the starting gate.

From this class was born a local screenwriting group. We paid dues, elected a president, put out a newsletter, expanded membership, flew in speakers from L.A., such as screenwriters, agency reps, UCLA screenwriting professors, screenplay analysts, and so on.

Based on the words these speakers had to impart I charted my own map into the film industry: write a great script, get it recognized, get a rewrite job, swing a deal, make a low-budget film from my own script, buy property in the Beverly Hills zip code.

Paul Schrader was my role model. His scripts for *Light Sleeper, Taxi Driver, Mishima, Hardcore* and *Raging Bull* were dog-eared and never far from reach.

Charlie Haas, the San Francisco-based writer of *Gremlins 2*, spoke to the group once where one person presented him with a three-act structure analysis of his film *Matinee.* "Wow, this is very fascinating," Haas said. "You know, I've got to pick up one of these books and read about this three-act structure thing because I have no idea what it is. I've never understood why a film can only have three acts. Why can't it have five acts or six acts? What I do is I just write and make sure that something is happening all the time on every page."

At these meetings, when someone mentioned they were writing something the first questions would be, "What's your log line?" "What's your inciting moment?" "How many pages is your first act?" There were lots of textbook discussions about structure, but very few people were doing any actual writing.

The handful of scripts that were written suffered from:

- Too much dialogue
- Not enough sex
- Implausible endings
- Not enough sex
- Lack of anything original
- Not enough sex

In truth, I've never been interested in screenwriting by itself. I've only been interested in writing scripts for films that I wanted to make.

Jumping ahead a few years, after I'd made the short film *Power* with Michael Dryhurst I was burning to take the leap to make my own feature film. I'd already started writing *Year* but knew it would be six months to a year before I'd have a finished script and I was impatient. I put blurbs in the newsletters of local writers' groups, "Looking for a finished script, book or short story that could be made into a feature film. Cannot have any scenes involving driving, fistfights or any physical action where someone could be injured. No explosions, no gunshots." I find action scenes always look phony in no-budget movies and didn't want any situations where somebody could be hurt and sue me.

Two writers responded. One story involved an auto race and mud football. The other was a romantic comedy set aboard a cruise ship in the Mediterranean. Based on those responses, as well as the scripts from the writers' group I was a member of, I now regard people who only want to write screenplays as unrealistic.

"All These Crappy Camcorder Movies"

Most locally made D.I.Y. movies have a bad rap and most of them deserve it. Most are little more than extended 90-minute Youtube videos made by people to entertain themselves and their friends.

These movies mostly suffer from:

- Too much dialogue
- Campy overacting
- Contrived reactions shots
- Endless bad movie clichés, comeback lines & one-upmanship
- Too much dialogue about the main characters and their problems
- Still more dialogue—Talk, talk, talk. People talking about everything they're doing, thinking and feeling.

The big reason these crappy camcorder movies don't go anywhere (aside from their amateurish technical flaws) is that they're not grounded in the real world and don't express any original ideas.

Don't make a film, short or feature, for the audience at your local film festival. Make it for audiences outside your zip code in the rest of the world. That's where the money is.

Have something new to say. Tell your own story. Cinema is always looking for new filmmakers with a new voice telling new stories that no one has heard of or seen before.

When I write a script that will take a year or more to make I ask myself these questions:

If someone else was making this would I want to see it?
Will it hold my own interest over the next year or two?

When You Get An Idea—Write It Down

EVERYBODY HAS THEIR OWN WAY OF WORKING. What follows isn't the only way but it's what works for me.

When I get ideas they happen all at once, like a big bang. I don't carry them around in my head, I write 'em down in as much detail as I can. Dialogue, shots, scenes, ideas, anything, everything. I find that one idea generates the next idea. So I write everything down, even if much of it doesn't make it into the final script.

I don't follow the screenwriting rules of writing scenes on 3x5 cards, pinning them on a board, moving them around, working up an outline and a treatment and so on. I just write. I don't worry about starting at the beginning and following through in chronological order. I just write whatever comes to me first. A bit of dialogue but no scene for it yet, I write it down. Character profiles, shot sequences, whole scenes, establishing shots, anything, I write 'em down.

In the middle of the night when I wake up and my head is exploding with ideas I know that if I go back to sleep I'll lose 'em all. (No matter how much we tell ourselves we'll remember it all the morning.) I'll pull out the laptop and start typing. I have notepads in my car, by my bed, in my coat pocket and in the bathroom. At work on a break or at lunch the laptop will be open and I'll be pecking away.

The quicker I get these ideas written down in the computer the sooner fresh ones flow in to take their place. Just when I think, "That's it, I'm done, I can't think of anything more," within a few minutes the ideas start coming again. In the early stages of a story I write in any style -- screenplay, treatment, bullet point notes, short story -- as long as I'm putting words on pages.

The hardest part of any kind of writing is filling the empty space with words. Writing in this loose way allows the writing process to be freer and vastly less intimidating.

Once I've got 100-200 pages I'll start arranging them into a rough script or "scriptment."

James Cameron's *"Scriptment"* Method

James Cameron writes his first drafts in a style he calls a "scriptment"—an amalgam of screenplay and an elaborate treatment that reads almost like a novel and is nearly as long. The scriptment for *Titanic* was 167 pages. His scriptment for *Strange Days* has been published and can be found on-line.

Cameron starts at the beginning and writes as much and as fast as he can all the way through to the end. If he has a scene fully thought out with action and dialogue he writes it out in screenplay form. If there's just an idea for a scene but it's not too specific yet he'll simply write a description of what he does know. He'll write out the dialogue that he has or simply says two people are talking about this and that.

Everything Cameron knows about the movie he writes down in his scriptment, effectively becoming a loose first draft or detailed conceptual draft of the script. Whatever he doesn't have written out in detail in the scriptment he knows he'll figure out by the time he starts polishing it into his formal first draft.

> Stanley Kubrick wrote the first draft of *Full Metal Jacket* as a short novel. Paddy Chayefsky's treatment for *Altered States* was so detailed that it was published as a novel and became a bestseller.

No Scene Cards & No Storyboards

I don't do scene cards or storyboards. I don't have anything against them. I just can't draw. I will, though, write out detailed shots for scenes into the script. When I write a scene and can see it in very specific camera angles I don't hesitate to write them in detail in the script. That said, when it finally comes time to shoot the scene I don't feel any obligation to stick to any of those shots.

> David Lean was so thorough that he wrote all his shots, sound effects and music cues into his scripts. His screenplay for *A Passage To India* is so detailed that at first glance you'd think it's a post-production continuity script.

Screenwriting Software

I've written with Word Perfect, Microsoft Word, Movie Magic Screenwriter and currently Final Draft.

I was a very reluctant convert to screenwriting software but now I find it invaluable in organizing all my random notes and scenes into the various drafts of a script.

I write in a production draft, meaning that every scene and location is numbered. This gives me an idea of the logistics of the script. If my first draft is 80 pages and there are 400 scenes then I know I've got a lot of condensing to do.

"Designing" The Film

When I start thinking about a new film I spend a lot of time thinking about how I want to approach it stylistically and technically: handheld or on tripod or with dolly shots; shooting in medium 2-shots versus lots of close-ups; jagged editing or longer holding shots; using natural light or coming up with a lighting pattern. I call this the "Design" of the film.

I also think in terms of an emotional map of the story and how I want the audience to be reacting, the peaks and valleys of the drama and where to add levity and give the audience a breather.

Stanley Kubrick & Opening Shots

How many times have we seen a movie open with a close-up of an alarm clock going off, a hand reaching over, fumbling to turn it off, then showing the main character in bed. Simple, easy, and seen it a thousand times.

Stanley Kubrick never did anything we'd ever seen before. He'd take great lengths to find new roads to take the audience down. I don't think anybody was better at opening shots that were symbolic of what the entire film was about than Stanley Kubrick:

2001: A Space Odyssey

We start out in black, then move upwards behind something curved to discover that we were looking at the dark side of the Moon. We continue rising up and see the Earth and the Sun beyond. Under this, the foreboding music of Thus Spake Zarathustra has been building, finally reaching a crescendo, at which point the title appears across the screen in bold white letters. We know from this very first shot that we are in for an epic journey through the solar system.

A Clockwork Orange

Cuts straight out of black to an extreme close-up of Alex's eye with exaggerated false eyelashes, then slowly zooms out and dollies back to reveal Alex and his droogs in the Korova Milk Bar. You know in this first shot that you are among some scary dudes in a weird world and that this guy is what it's all about for the next two hours.

Full Metal Jacket

Opens in a boot camp barber shop with a series of identical close shots of new recruits' heads getting buzzed, being sheared of their identity so that by the end of the sequence they are all the same and ready for the drill instructor to mass produce them into Marines.

Eyes Wide Shut

Opens on a wide shot as Nicole Kidman slips off a black party dress revealing herself to be completely nude except for a pair of black high heels. Unquestionably, the greatest opening shot in the history of cinema. (It's the screensaver on my laptop!) From the first image you know this film is about eroticism and fantasy.

Using the openings of Kubrick's films as a model my opening sequence in *Year* centered around a calendar so that the audience would know right off the bat that this is a story about the passage of time.

Writing Basics—Beginning, Middle & End

Everything in between is the "middle." This is where most of the movie takes place. With a two-hour movie the "middle" can take up 65-100 minutes of that. In script terms that's roughly 70-80%. This is also where most movies get lost. The main thing is to figure out what your story is about and start directing everything towards that.

There are a million books about writing, yet I've found that most successful writers have never read any of them. They just write and try to keep their stories interesting and never boring.

> **You'll never know what kind of writer you are until you start writing.**

Plan Your Script To Have A Killer Ending

As important as how your movie starts is how it ends. It must be an ending that leaves the audience with an impact, in a state of euphoria or weeping buckets.

An Officer And A Gentleman
I'll watch this whole movie just for the emotional impact of that great final freeze-frame.

Silence Of The Lambs
The last shot when Hannibal Lecter tells Clarice over the phone, "I'm having an old friend for dinner," then watching him head off after his next victim. You can't help but feel great about life.

Forrest Gump
Tom Hanks puts his son, whom he's only just met, onto the school bus, then sits down to wait for him to come home. He turns his head, there's a gust of wind, a feather flies up into the air, the camera pulls up and the music swells.

Field Of Dreams
Ray Liotta is walking off towards rows of corn. Kevin Costner calls after him, "Wait. You said if I built it you would come." Liotta turns and says, "I said, if you build it *he* will come," and nods to the catcher still on the field. Only then does Costner realize that the catcher is his father. Costner steps closer to the man and says, "Dad . . . you wanna play catch?" We see the two men, father and son, tossing the baseball as the camera pulls away in a helicopter shot, revealing the headlights of cars full of people coming to watch. The music swells and the camera continues to pull away, revealing the line of cars stretching off for miles. Every time I see this I think of my father who is no longer with me.

The morning after this aired on network television I was in an electronics store that had a tape of this playing on every TV on the shelves. I had to crouch down so no one could see the tears streaming down my cheeks.

Script Length Rule: A Page A Minute—Don't Believe It

The studio standard script length back in the 1940s was 140-160 pages. In the 1960s dialogue became more condensed and scripts tightened to 120-130 pages; then went to 120 pages in the 1970s. By the early 90s it was down to 100 pages. Now it's around 85-90 pages.

The first thing an agent or producer does with a new script is flip to the last page to see how long it is. (I do the same thing.) The shorter the script, the more likely someone's going to read it. Though, more likely, they'll give it to an entry-level reader first.

Tight. Spare. Direct. Keep the words as lean as possible. Paul Schrader doesn't even write "and" in his description, he just uses commas.

My screenplay for *Year* was 129 pages and had 400 scenes. Much of that was due to my use of numbered scene headings for shots and other details for keeping my footage organized for the editing. The script also contained a lot of technical notes to myself on sound cues, shot lists, editing ideas, etc. I have a terrible memory so I put all my notes in the script, details I would never include in a "spec script" for somebody else but which I feel justified including as the writer-director in a "shooting script."

When the editing of *Year* was finally finished I went back through the script and cut out everything that wasn't used. That 129 page script for the 109 minute movie went down to just 79 pages.

Francis Ford Coppola's script for *The Godfather*, a three hour movie, is 150 pages. Using the "one page per minute" formula, that should be a 2½-hour movie. Coppola actually filmed all 150 pages, making a 4½-hour movie. Of the three-hour *Godfather* that was released, which received the Oscar for Best Picture and is now considered the best movie ever made, only 100 pages of Coppola's script appear on the screen. One hundred pages = three hours = 1/3 of a page per minute.

I now regard a screenplay as nothing more than 75+ pages of story to get me to the set.

Complicated Action & White Space

When I look at a page dense with detailed action my first reaction is, "Man, that's a lot of stuff to shoot. Is all this really necessary?" Also, a page dense with narrative action in large block paragraphs makes the reading more time-consuming.

Make it visually easier on the eyes by keeping the sentences short and double-spacing between each one. This will make the scene read faster. Of course, it will also take up more space on the page.

Readers and producers like a sparsely written page with lots of white space—the double-spacing between location headings, narrative action and dialogue—because the reading goes faster. Also, as most scripts are terrible, it helps to ease the pain.

Titles—Keep 'em Short

The first thing people see when they pick up a script, look through a film festival roster or even just when looking through the paper for what's playing around town, is the title. Every film needs a great title. The cooler the title, the higher the audience interest.

Short titles work best. Two or three words or a name. *Rocky. The Deer Hunter. Crash. The Killing Fields. Death Proof. Serpico. Annie Hall. Boogie Nights. Manhattan. Dog Day Afternoon.* Fail Safe.

Long titles are confusing. *The Englishman Who Walked Up A Hill And Came Down A Mountain. The Effect Of Gamma Rays On Man In The Moon Marigolds. I Never Cried For My Father.* Most of these were plays where titles work differently. As film titles go, they're kind of baffling.

Think Of Your Title Alphabetically

When Bonnie and I went to the San Francisco Independent Film Festival (also known as "Indiefest") we couldn't wait to see the film catalogue with our movie in it. It was a very nice catalogue with a detailed schedule with screening times, venues where all the films were playing and a personalized description of each film listed alphabetically. Our film *Year* was listed dead last.

In video stores, most people instinctively start at the A's and work their way down the aisle. Think about it, how often do you make it to the W's or the Y's before you've picked out a movie or two? I'm considering re-titling our film to *A Year* before putting it out on DVD so it'll move to the front of the line.

Locations—Keep 'em Easy

Locations are killers in no-budget filmmaking. Keep most of your action in private homes and apartments. When casting find actors who'll let you film where they live. This will keep the location process more "in the family."

Likewise with business locations. If a character works in an office or restaurant see if you can shoot there and work that into the story. Otherwise, work your scenes to use public places like parks and sidewalks where you can shoot with just your actors, yourself and a handheld camera without attracting attention. Shooting in an urban area on a Sunday also helps as it tends to be quieter.

Don't write scenes set in Costco, McDonald's, Best Buy, J.C. Penney, a 76 gas station and so on. These are corporate entities and you will *never* get permission to use them. If you must shoot in a business or restaurant stick to ones that are small and privately owned, such as a clothing boutique, a coffee shop or diner, where getting permission to film during or after hours could be simpler.

You might be asking yourself whether you need to worry about your locations now while you're writing, instead of just waiting and dealing with all that later when you're getting closer to production. The answer is no. When writing a no-budget film you have to be conscious of your limitations every step of the way.

"I love making movies, but I hate writing."

I know aspiring writers who say they hate the writing process so they only do a first draft of a script and call it done until some producer buys it and tells them how it should be rewritten. I tell them that will never happen because they haven't done the work. Of course, they don't listen to me. Also, of course, nobody's bought one of their crappy first drafts.

If you absolutely hate writing then don't do it. It's one thing for an accomplished writer to say they hate the work, but if you haven't accomplished anything then don't worry about it. Nobody says you have to be a writer. No one's pounding on your door to read your unproofed pages. The world will continue turning without you. This isn't a requirement of the DMV to keep your driver's license renewed or to retain your citizenship status. Write because you want to and because you have to. Writing and moviemaking takes a lot of work. Other people will write their scripts and get their films made. If you aren't committed to putting in the time and the sweat then nobody's going to twist your arm.

> Writing isn't fun or easy. It's work. If I don't do it then it won't get done. Nobody else is going to do it for me. It is, however, satisfying when you finish a project and can look at it and say unapologetically, "I did this." It's important to enjoy that because it may be the only reward you will ever get.

Originally planned to be the opening shot of *Year*, it ultimately didn't appear until twenty minutes into the movie.

Writing Year

I INTENTIONALLY WANTED *YEAR* TO HAVE A LARGE CAST. Since I was making a film with actors who'd mostly never made a feature film before, I didn't want any actor to feel that they'd have to carry the whole film by themselves. I also didn't want to make a one-character profile, such as Billy Bob Thornton's *Sling Blade*, which would require an actor to be present every day of shooting, an extremely demanding request to make of someone who'd be giving me their spare time. Instead, I designed the film to have multiple characters so that each actor would be asked to commit no more than a few days or so spread out over the course of a year.

I also wasn't sure that I was capable of telling a story about just two people that would hold an audience's attention for an hour and a half. With a multi-character story I could have overlapping story lines. This way, if one story wasn't appealing to someone in the audience, within a minute or two we'd be onto another story they might like better. I wanted to keep the scenes short and moving to not bore the audience.

Finally, I overwrote the film intentionally. I knew that not all of the 139 page 400 scene script would make it into the final film. Before we ever started shooting I anticipated that the film would play too long and need to be cut down. I wanted to give myself enough options so that in the final edit I would only use the shots and scenes and performances that absolutely worked and stood out. Anything that didn't work or didn't work well enough would be cut. Of course, exactly what would or wouldn't work I wouldn't know until after everything had been shot and edited.

The Stone sisters in *Year*, Ava (Bonnie Bennett), Sydney (Christine Nicholson), Gina (Katherine Pappa) and Vivian (Carol Miranda).

Year opens with an elaborate New Year's Eve party scene with almost every character in the film under the same roof. My version of the *Godfather* and *Deer Hunter* wedding sequences. I wanted the film to open with a bang. In this case, the pop of champagne corks.

The first version of the script started with voices counting, "Five! . . . Four! . . . Three! . . . Two! . . . One!" Then cut straight out of black to a room full of people shouting, "Happy New Year!" I wanted the film to span from the first second of the new year to the last second of the year, cutting straight to black again at the end.

I gave this draft to my wife Bonnie and friend Michael Dryhurst, who both said: "You open the movie with a twenty page party scene. Who are these people? I don't know anything about them. They all run together. It's confusing trying to keep track of who is who."

Friend and filmmaking partner, writer-producer-director Michael Dryhurst. Golden Globe-winning producer and Academy Award Best Picture nominee with John Boorman for *Hope And Glory*. Also one of the best natural actors I've ever worked with.

In the next draft I started the movie just after the last sunset of New Year's Eve and proceeded to a series of quick scenes where each character telegraphed something about themselves in cinematic shorthand:

- The workaholic sister is introduced in her office
- The neurotic sister is seen trying on a new sweater and not being satisfied
- The alcoholic mother with terminal cancer is seen having a spasm of pain, then knocking back prescription pills with a shot of vodka

The device I used to connect all these different women together as being members of the same dysfunctional family was to end this series of short introductory scenes with each woman, from the matriarch all the way down to the nine year old granddaughter, saying "Fuck it" to themselves.

Get real criticism. I always say, "Don't be nice. Be honest."

Towards the end of *Year* is a sequence where Doris Stone (Hazel Bell), the matriarch of the family, is succumbing to cancer and her four adult daughters gather around in a deathwatch. This was much longer in script and, odd as it may sound, contained quite a bit of comedy. I'd based this on the experiences I had during the deathwatch for my own mother. If you've ever been through the situation of waiting around for someone to die you know that weird things happen.

For example, my mother's final days were spent in a coma on a rented hospital bed in the middle of my brother's living room with a morphine drip feeding into her veins. Her body had been consumed by cancer and she was never going to open her eyes again. Days passed as we stayed close by in the living room, eating pizza and microwaved lasagna and watching TV. My mother loved *Colombo* and, of all things, A&E was running a *Colombo* marathon. For days we sat watching Peter Falk annoy his suspects as our mother withered away before us.

I wanted to incorporate some of that bizarreness into the deathwatch sequence and created a series of scenes of the sisters getting hooked watching reruns of an old vampire movie, to the point that they are laughing and yelling things at the screen while their mother lies comatose just a few feet away. It was a joyful scene of a dysfunctional family finally unifying in an absurd way.

We shot the death sequence over the course of a day and a half on a Saturday and Sunday. That particular scene was shot near the end of the first day. We were all tired and, quite frankly, I shot the scene too quickly, not giving it the time it deserved, and could never get it to work convincingly enough in the editing. It was like watching a movie that was going fine in one direction, then suddenly changed gears and veered off somewhere else.

I worked on the sequence and reworked it and reworked it some more until it finally became painfully clear that it did not fit. In fact, the more I looked at those scenes the clearer it became that they should probably be a separate movie of their own.

In the end I wound up using only a handful of the deathwatch scenes, dropping all the humor entirely and focusing exclusively on the dramatic scenes that propelled the film towards its finale.

You never really know what's going to work until the whole movie's cut together.

Sample Script Pages

WHENEVER I LOOK THROUGH A BOOK THAT DISCUSSES SCREENWRITING I always feel cheated if it doesn't include samples of the author's own work. No, it's more than that—I get really pissed off. So that I don't get you pissed off with me, I'm including a couple pages from *Year* and *Nightbeats*.

The one feature of my writing style that's evolved as a result of working with actors is that I write less description for what the actors need to do and for how they should deliver the dialogue. If anything, I may be more inclined to write something of what they may be thinking or feeling to give the actor a reference for how they might approach a scene. I've had such wonderful experiences with actors that I truly enjoy giving a scene over to them, getting the camera rolling and seeing what they do with it.

I also hate seeing sample pages reformatted or changed in any way so these are actual scans of pages from my scripts. Once we're in production I'm constantly modifying and filling my scripts with editing notes and those are reflected on these pages.

A lot of people have the impression that no-budget D.I.Y. movies are just improvised on the spot, and maybe some are. If you want others to take your work seriously then you need to take it seriously as well. Write it all out just as if you were making a big Hollywood movie so that you know what you're making before you ever start looking for actors or turn the camera on.

Year 27   1-2-06   22*

6   <u>**INT   CARRE HOUSE   NIGHT   [SHOT - #52]**</u>   56*

HIGH WIDE SHOT: THE ROOM with everyone. Stroke of midnight -

    EVERYONE
    Happy New Year!

Shouts, laughter, hugs, kisses. Champagne corks.

-- Ava and Brendan - New Year's kisses, big smiles for crowd -
then go separate ways.

-- Sydney fleetingly kisses Miles.

-- Ava gives Lana a hug. Some looks between them of making up
after their exchange earlier.

-- Gina and Chris kiss.   *

-- John Cassavetes moves to give Joan a kiss. She turns her head   *
so his lips just miss hers and he kisses her cheek. Passionless.   *
Then she turns, giving her friends, big hugs and smiles. John   *
feels out of place.   *
                                                               *

-- Morris and Tracy share a friendly kiss.   *

-- Hugs and kisses are shared between Ava, Vivian, Doris, Sydney,
Miles, Gina and Chris -   *

-- David and Dina kiss -

-- Doris gives big kisses to every man she can get her hands on -

-- David approaches to Lana to kiss, but she turns away. Finds   *
herself facing John. Gives him a New Years kiss.   *

7   <u>**ANGLE   AVA, DORIS, VIVIAN, GINA, SYDNEY**</u>   57*

posed with glasses of champagne in a toast.   *

Brendan snaps a picture. Miles shooting with Vivian's camcorder.   *

The women sip their champagne. Doris theatrically downs her entire
glass and follows it with a vodka chaser.

7A <u>**ANGLE   CLOSE-UPS   LANA   [SHOT - #51]**</u>   57A*

Nursing a glass of champagne. Standing behind TWO WOMEN GUESTS   *
talking.   *

    WOMAN GUEST #1   *
    My God, what is it with you and men? Do they always   *
    have to be married?   *

First page of *Nightbeats*. Starting out with a visual grabber.

NIGHTBEATS

BLACK SCREEN

The sharp, distinct classical chords of a **DANCE STUDIO PIANO** playing for a ballet class / rehearsal. Then we begin to SEE --

BLACK & WHITE PHOTOGRAPHS

of a FIFTEEN YEAR-OLD GIRL (MERCY) in dance leotard and shoes in ballet poses. A portfolio of images of a serious, aspiring young ballerina.

THE DANCE STUDIO PIANO CONTINUING UNDER THIS --

BLACK SCREEN - TRANSITION

From the studio piano, now MIX TO : BLOOD-RUSHING, LOIN-ROUSING ELECTRO-GUITAR & DRUM ROCK --

A FLASH OF WHITE LIGHT, and --

POLE DANCING STAGE - INT. - NIGHT   [T#6]

OFF THE BLINDING SWEEP OF A STAGE LIGHT --

A STEEL POLE in center of stage. Shiny dark-colored plastic backdrop. Piercing spotlights. A DISCO BALL SHOWERING the room in horizontal raindrops of light. Then --

MERCY (mid-30's) -- emerges onto the stage to perform. At the top of her form. A star. A pro. An athlete. Wrapping herself around the pole the way every guy would want her to wrap herself around him. The center of this universe of body and movement, grinds, lust, desire. She's what every man in the audience wants. And she knows it. And she loves it. It fuels her. Deep inside she'd like to send every guy home with a stain in his pants. And she knows how to do it. She's voracious. She'll consume everything. Even herself...

BLACK SCREEN - TRANSITION

From the stripper rock, MIX TO : a lonely BOAT HORN. And SOFT LAPPING WATER...

P.O.V. - ROW OF BUILDINGS OF THE CITY - NIGHT [#33-34]

TELE - P.O.V. : A WALL OF LIT-UP BUILDINGS of the CITY SCAPE.

RIVERFRONT LOOKOUT - EXT. - NIGHT [T#]

BIG C.U. : A MATCH / LIGHTER IGNITING. FOLLOW the flame to the end of a cigarette. A lung-filling drag. Then we SEE the eyes, the face...

...Mercy. Time has passed. Hasn't been good to her..

P.O.V.-WATERRIPPLING   [TK33:34]
_____

Reflecting the lights from the city.

RIVERFRONTLOOKOUT-EXT.-NIGHT TK1
_____

SIDE ANGLE : Mercy sitting alone on a bench on an overlook of a river.

Redder than red lip gloss, leather jacket, cheap low-cut top, short skirt, black fishnets, spike heels/boots.*

> [*COSTUME NOTE : MERCY & CECE'S CLOTHES are all Frederick's-
> style clearance.]

O.S., SOUND : The tinkling of PIANO KEYS. The LEAD-IN to a SONG... low, sultry...

P.O.V.-BRIDGE SPANNING INTO CITY - NIGHT [TK33:34]
_____

> [NOTE : It is not intended for any of these shots to specifically be
> San Francisco, but a large urban city.]

HIGHWAY BRIDGE OVER WATER TO THE CITY - EXT. - NIGHT
_____

TRAVELING P.O.V.S - DRIVING : Crossing over a bridge spanning water toward the lighted buildings of a CITY SCAPE. A landscape of concrete, asphalt, brick, steel, glass. A hot summer night. Moon and silver-rimmed clouds reflected on glass buildings.

> [SHOOTING NOTES: Driving over Bay Bridge into San Francisco or
> Oakland.   Lit-up   buildings   against   night   ETC'S   to   fully   W
> establish.]

DUBOIS (V.O.)
There's no place lonelier than a city at night. Big, empty.
Millions of lights in the windows representing millions of
different people, but out on the streets you'd never know
there was a soul left in the world. Like one of those sci-
fi movies from the 50's where the bomb's been dropped
and everybody's gone. Just a handful of ghosts left to
haunt the shadows. The bomb might as well have gone
off, everything's closed anyway. Almost everything. You
can still get a drink, or whatever your pleasure is.

-- *Street night shots*

DUBOIS (V.O.)
Day people work their lives to be somebody. Night people
exis between the cracks. Under the radar. World without
sun. Where dreams have gone... Be in a room full of people,
you're always alone...

Rewriting—The Most Important Writing You'll Ever Do

"Brevity being the soul of wit"
Hamlet, William Shakespeare

ONCE I GET A SCRIPT ALL WORKED OUT FROM "FADE IN" TO "FADE OUT" the real work and the fun of writing begins. I'll start at page one, editing and rewriting scenes, cleaning up sentences so they flow smoothly, correcting punctuation, reviewing and cutting every word I can, shaping this jumble into a solid, credible screenplay. I'll do this process several times before ever showing it to my wife Bonnie, who is always my first and best critic.

To be a professional you must be coldly objective about your own work. You must be ruthless. Everything must make sense and be plausible. The script must be bullet proof.

In this phase of the writing I often imagine the script is a rough cut of a film that runs four or five hours and that I'm an editor brought in to pare it down to a lean 90 minutes. I start by skimming off the fat:

- If there's a group of seven friends who hang out together, try cutting them down to five, or four, or three, or two.
- If something is said in ten lines condense it down to five, or four, or one. Or maybe just a shot.
- Think about how much the scenes will cost to shoot. After all, every penny is coming out of your pocket.

Cut To The Chase

All those scenes of someone driving, pulling up, getting out of the car, walking into a house, entering the living room, saying, "Hi." "Hi, how are you?" "I'm fine. How was your day." And on and on. Look at these scenes from the point of view of a production manager calculating the time that will be required to shoot all these shots leading up to the scene that you really want to get to in the first place. What do you absolutely need? Can you save time—yours, the actors' and the audience's—and just cut straight to the main scene itself?

Every word or scene that I cut makes the remaining words and scenes better.

> On the cinematic highway, tickets are only handed out when you're moving too slow.

The Simpler A Scene Is To Read The Easier It Will Be To Film

It's one thing to fill up pages as a writer dreaming up a story. It's quite another when you're the one who's going to shoot them.

A complicated scene that isn't pulled off smoothly will come off as confusing, showing your weakness as a filmmaker and will make the film look amateurish. It will also prevent it from getting into a festival.

Play The Masters In The Background

Sometimes during this part I'll have DVD's of my favorite movies playing in the background, like Paul Schrader's *Light Sleeper,* or Hal Ashby's *The Landlord, Bound For Glory or The Last Detail.* Filmmakers who told their stories through images and ambiguity, kept the dialogue spare and elliptical, with characters who don't tell the story as much as make you observe it, and who speak volumes without ever uttering a word. I'll look from these movies to my pages and ask myself, "What would Paul Schrader or Hal Ashby do here?"

Clean Up The Script Before Sending It Out

The script must excite actors to want to be a part of the film for the days or months that it will take to make without any promise of financial reward. Actors train studying the great plays of Arthur Miller, Tennessee Williams and David Mamet. They know good writing from slop. Make your pages as polished as they can be.

   BOTTOM LINE: Rewrite. Rewrite. Rewrite.

Jon Roe—Writing The Easy Way

WHEN I WORKED IN KANSAS I DID A LOT OF TRAVELING WITH REPORTER JON ROE, who had been a newspaper reporter and columnist for over twenty years before making a switch to television. Writing was always a favorite topic of conversation between us and one time he told me how he'd written a special weekend section for the newspaper, which was the equivalent of a 400-page book, in just six weeks. His method was so unconventional and yet so simple that I tried applying it to my own writing habits and found it to be incredibly effective and productive. Almost twenty years after Jon told me this story I called him up to share his method for this book:

JON ROE: The annual Kansas Day edition of the *Wichita Eagle-Beacon* always had a lot of different articles and I said, "Why don't we do something that represents Kansas instead of just doing a bunch of stories about how the oil industry looks this year and how farm crops look this year. Let's take a city dweller and country dweller, sort of the two aspects of the state, and go back in their past to when they settled and show how the state was formed by these two forces."

Everybody said, "No, no, not interested."

So I had to go up to the Kansas State Historical Society and research, find my people, go out and talk to them, do some interviews. Then I came back and met with the advertising department and convinced them that this was doable, that they could sell ads and what kind of ads they could sell. If you can show them they can make money then they'll let you do it.

And boom! They said, "Okay, go ahead."

And this book had to be essentially three or four hundred typewritten pages in order to fill all of this space in the newspaper and you basically just went home for four or five weeks, wrote it there and turned the pages in weekly?

That's right, I did. I turned it in weekly even though it all ran at the same time. I would give them a section each week so they could get the different sections set in type.

It's exactly the way Charles Dickens wrote many of his novels. They were serialized. It's not that difficult if you view the piece in sections and say, "Okay, here's the beginning. I'm gonna have three sections in the middle and here's the end."

So that's how I did it. Luckily, when they got it all set in type I was able to go through it and essentially proofread it. But, actually, I did more than proofread it. I made quite a few changes.

It took about four or five sections of the Sunday paper to tell the whole story.

Organization for a writer of anything has to be, "I know where I want to start, I know where I want to end and I pretty much know how I want to get there. I want to do it in this many chapters and I want to hit these high spots. Okay, now I start writing."

Once you've outlined it that way you can write anywhere. If you're bored with something in the first part then you can say, "Aw, the hell with it. I'm gonna write the ending. I love this ending." You don't have to put off writing the ending until you've slogged all the way through the story. That helped me write a great deal faster than I would have otherwise. If you get bogged down in the middle and say, "Oh, God, this is terrible. I don't know why I ever started writing this thing." Well, if you start feeling that way you're not going to write very well so go off and write some other part.

You shouldn't be editing while you're writing the first draft. If you're editing while you're writing you're not allowing yourself any creativity. You're looking at everything you're putting down on the page and thinking, "Hmm . . . will that really fit? Is that any good?" Don't do that. Just write like crazy and get all the stuff out there. You edit when you're all through and you start the cutting process and the polishing process and all that.

Your conscious mind is a problem solver, but it's not creative. Your subconscious is the creative one. That has to do with writing something and then if you get to someplace where you're stuck or it's not very exciting and you don't know whether you ought to go this way or that then stop and go do something else. Eat breakfast or mow the lawn and don't think about it because your subconscious will be working on it. Your subconscious is so creative. It can do anything. If you just give it time, when you come back, chances are ninety-nine to one that your subconscious will have worked out the problem and off you go again.

Another thing that saved me in writing was understanding that I shouldn't be paying much conscious attention to what I was putting down in that first draft. Somebody once said nothing really good is ever written—it's rewritten. That's pretty much true.

When you go through it the second time that's when your conscious mind starts analyzing and making judgments. It's very much, I would guess, like cutting a film where you're throwing away things that don't fit and marking things that do, that really turn you on, that you need to do some more with. The more you do this the better your work gets.

Somebody also said that no work of art is ever really done, it's abandoned. At some point you've got to say, "I'm through. I'm through writing. I'm through editing. It's done."

That's sort of how I did that, and still do when I'm writing a book. Before I had a computer I would tear the pages out in little sheets and put them on the floor in chronological order. Now with computers, of course, it's very easy to do. I just move them around until they all fit and make sense and before you know it you've got the book written. It's very sloppy, of course. It's emotion, it's feeling, what you want to say to the world. When you start part two, the editing phase, you make it slick and pretty and appealing and powerful.

A tape recorder helped me a great deal. One of those little ones you carry around with you. I found that when I was driving to work or driving out to cover an assignment I would dictate parts of the book into the tape recorder then type them out at night. I'd get three, four, five pages of stuff. It's particularly easy to do when you're dictating dialogue. You hear the dialogue in your head so you may as well talk it into the tape recorder and that's work you don't have to do that night. You just type it up.

To me, it's a good deal looser, freer, more immediate. Writing is nothing more than telling a person something. All that other stuff about style and technique is pretty much bullshit.

We've got to convince ourselves that there's nothing special about the drivel we're putting on these pages. It's a first draft, you know. Once we understand that all we're doing is a very, very rough draft, that we're going to "write" when we come to the second draft, then we can just go crazy.

I think about different rules in writing magazines like, "Set aside three hours a night to be productive." I tried that and found myself dreading that time. What struck me so much about how you wrote this massive project in a short period of time was how you would start the day by writing a little until you couldn't think of anything more, then go and have some coffee, come back and think up something else. You spread it out over the course of the day and by that night you'd have ten pages or so.

If you realize you have all day to write, and not that little one hour in the morning or two hours in the evening, then it's okay to write one paragraph and stop and go do something else. That's one paragraph you don't have to write that night.

When you're writing something big that you believe in you're always writing it. It's in your head all the time. And when you're getting all these ideas in your head all the time why in the world wait until ten o'clock at night to put it on paper? Particularly with smaller and smaller laptops and dictation software. You can write something down all the time. Whether you're riding the bus or subway or when you're eating your lunch.

When I was working for the newspaper I would have a sandwich and write my own stuff on the lunch hour. Rather than go with the guys and talk about writing, which is a lot of fun but really doesn't do much. And I would get incredible amounts of writing done. We know what we need to know about writing and that is that you've got to sit down and write. And that doesn't mean an hour at the end of the day. It means every little chance you get.

Now when I finish a manuscript I show it to my wife and give it to a friend who knows what good writing is as opposed to someone who is just going to say nice things. What do you do?

I generally rewrite it before I show it to anybody, then I'll show it to my wife who is highly, highly critical. She knows she doesn't have to fake anything. She's also a writer and understands that writers are always hanging onto stuff because they love how it sounds. And most of the time that's the stuff that needs to be thrown out.

I listen to her suggestions and then I rewrite again. I'll rewrite it maybe three or four times before I finally say, "Goddammit, I'm tired of this story! Get the thing out there. Get it published or something."

I've found that if I write the end early on it helps me think more clearly about how I'm going to get there.

That's correct, that's correct. The wonderful thing about writing is that you may go off totally on a new tangent. You can't predict that. You don't know what's going to happen. You can't even control it. And that's the fun. That's why I never like to outline too closely on the first draft.

You know, I've never done an outline. I find that once I get doing it I don't want to be constricted.

You know, F. Scott Fitzgerald decided, "I'm gonna go to Hollywood and I'm gonna figure out all the rules and I'm gonna write exactly what they want and make a million." And he was a total failure in Hollywood. So the whole idea of following the rules and doing something fabulous is just total bullshit. I don't believe it. I think the films that have really, really been great have not followed those rules.

Yeah, the breakout movies are generally made by people who are following their own rules. I tell people that you can't think about what other people are doing, you've got to follow your own voice because people are always looking for what's new, what's different, and you've got to make yourself stand out.

And trust your subconscious. Let it get out there and show you some things. You can always refine it when you're rewriting. But let it sing, so to speak. I see the Arts all together as an amalgam. I see people who are great musicians or great artists or writers as being able to move around in the Arts, because it's all creativity.

I think God is creation. Creativity is good, destruction is bad, and artists exist to create. As long as you're creating I think that's what it's all about.

Also, the more you write, the more you write. You don't have a finite amount of creativity in you. You renew it the more you do it.

Summing Up: No-Budget Screenwriting Do's & Don'ts

WRITING DO'S—WRITE SOMETHING YOU CAN MAKE. Look at what you have available to you and develop a film around a slice of life you know about:

- That can be filmed without money (beyond the acquisition of a camera, computer, etc.)
- That can be filmed in your own house and the homes of your actors
- With dialogue that actors can speak and perform

WRITING DON'TS—DON'T WRITE WHAT YOU CAN'T AFFORD. You're not a studio. You don't have a budget. So don't write scenes that you can't do and will only cause you problems:

- Action sequences and car chases. People can be injured and the filmmaker is liable.
- Lots of Dialogue. You're making a film, not a play.
- Long Scenes. The longer the scene, the more time it will take to film. Continuity becomes an issue. Break long scenes down into shorter scenes.
- Locations you can't get access to.

COMEDY WRITING WARNING—COMEDY IS ONE OF THE HARDEST THINGS TO PULL OFF. Just look at how many major studio comedies tank, in spite of all the highly paid professionals at their disposal. No-budget comedy is incredibly tough. There are classic exceptions: *Clerks* and *Swingers*. But don't take my word for it, just go to any local film festival playing locally produced shorts and experience it for yourself. Most people's personal sense of humor does not translate well to a large audience. But if you're still determined to make a comedy, at least do your audience a favor and keep the following bad-comedy bits out of your movie:

- Rolling of the eyes
- Head shakes
- Shoulder shrugs
- Comeback lines
- Dialogue one-upmanship

- Goofy sidekick characters who exist only to provide comic relief[4]
- Goofy lines
- Goofy clothes
- Any character who exists solely to support the main character and does not have a real life of their own

FILMING NOTE: If you must shoot a comedy protect yourself by shooting scenes with several angles and multiple close-ups. You're going to need these if the comedy doesn't work and comes across as clumsy or trite. With a variety of different angles you can cut these "bad" reactions out.

---

4 Such as Hugh Grant's roommate in *Notting Hill*, who wears strange clothes, says odd things and is completely off the wall. Why on earth would Hugh Grant share his house with this nut case?

CASTING: Finding Actors

Filming Hazel Bell and Carol Miranda with the natural light coming in through the windows for *Year*

Actors As Artistic Partners

I MAKE A PROMISE TO THE ACTORS: "Whether you've made a film with someone else before or not, I promise you this will be the one film you make that you'll be proud of and will show to people as an example of what you do."

When people first start getting excited about filmmaking, learning about cameras, lighting and editing, the one thing nobody stops to think about is the most important element of a movie: the actors. Beginning filmmakers (and quite a few big-time ones) look upon actors as enigmas expected to turn on a dime, hit their marks and emote on cue.

Movies are *nothing* without actors. You can have the world's best script and the most stunning cinematography but if the people on the screen can't act you're dead.

No Hollywood movie can be made without movie star names above the title. Look no further than today's movie posters: huge close-ups of stars' faces and little else. Back in the sixties the poster for a war movie would be a finely detailed artist's illustration of action scenes, explosions, men charging, tanks firing. Now it's just a star's grizzled face beneath a helmet.

> John Huston (*The Maltese Falcon, Fat City*) used to say that once he'd cast the film his job was pretty much over. I never understood until I made my first film how true that is.

Prepping to shoot wife Bonnie Bennett's monologue for the radio interview scene in our living room for *Year*. One of the rules we established in the casting process was that if an actor was cast, their home could be used as a location. In keeping with our rules, our house was a primary location.

Marrying Into The Theatre

I was very fortunate to have married one of the most incredible actors I've ever seen. From the moment I saw Bonnie on stage I knew she had enormous on-screen potential so I channeled all my energy into getting her clothes off.

(I can't recommend this for everybody, but as an unpaid filmmaker it's a great perk.)

Bonnie and I got together when she was in Sacramento's most successful stage show, *Six Women With Brain Death*, a musical comedy about women's issues with a cast of five other incredibly talented women, some of whom played the parts of Bonnie's character's sisters in *Year*.

From the very start there was no question that Bonnie would play one of the main parts in *Year*. If nothing else I knew she would be the one member of the cast who'd show up.

Get One Good Actor & The Rest Will Follow

I've made two feature length films and have not held any casting calls or any auditions.

I've been to casting calls for films that friends were making and I think they're largely a waste of time. It's almost impossible to tell what an actor is capable of when they come into a room full of strangers and do a cold reading from pages they've only just been handed. How an actor looks and how well they speak is not going to convey any real sense of how they can act, meaning how they inhabit a role.

There's only one way to find out how an actor acts and that's by going to plays. A beginning filmmaker cannot base their understanding of acting by what they've seen on TV and movies. It's fine if you're casting in L.A. but pointless if you're in Chattanooga. Good actors do theatre. Look in the newspaper for the best reviewed plays around town and that's where you'll find good actors.

When you find an actor who would be ideal for one of the roles in your film, approach them, tell them what you have in mind and give them a script. If they're willing to join you then the rest of your casting is pretty much done.

Good theatre actors are used to doing lots of different plays with lots of different actors. You'll be asked, "Who do you have in mind for the other parts?" If you respond, "I don't know yet. Do you have any ideas?" you'll find that actors like working with other good actors and will probably know all the other good actors in the area. Actors don't want to play opposite someone who's lazy, difficult or untalented. They'll only suggest people who'll be dependable, show up on time and know their lines.

When Bonnie and I were gathering our cast for *Year*, if one of our actors said, "I know someone who'd be good for this part," Bonnie and I would invite them over to the house. If they'd been doing theater for a while and came recommended we didn't need to see them audition, we could tell by their personality what they were like and we'd go with our instincts.

Later when we were making the movie a few actors mentioned, "I was so surprised you never even wanted to hear me read. You just trusted me." This goes a long way toward creating trust with an actor.

You'll then have a company of actors who like to work with each other and all you have to do is stand back and let them do what they do.

During these initial visits I also told the actors the one thing I wanted from their performances: "I don't want to see any acting. I have to believe everything I'm watching. When you're in a scene with another actor I don't want to feel like I'm watching two actors. I want to feel like I'm watching two people."

They were all given copies of Michael Winterbottom's *Wonderland* as a reference to the film I wanted to make—handheld, natural light, wireless mics—and completely natural, understated acting.

If one of the actors should bring up some aspect of the script that isn't working for them, pay attention. They've typically played more characters than you can imagine and can tell when something doesn't ring true.

"I don't do theatre. I only do film."

Soon as I hear that I'm not interested. I believe in learning the ropes and doing your homework. Theatre actors are experienced. They're disciplined. Someone who says they only want to do films tells me they're not going to learn their lines and they're not going to show much depth in their performance, more akin to modeling poses and bad sitcom. They'll also probably show up late to the set.

BOTTOM LINE: Pass.

Nightbeats—Using Available Assets

Robert Rodriguez wrote the script for his no-budget film *El Mariachi* around the assets available to him—a small town in Mexico, a bus and a guitar.

John Cassavetes planned his self-financed films around his strongest asset -- his wife, actress Gena Rowlands.

The idea for *Nightbeats* was born when *Year* played in the San Francisco Independent Film Festival. Looking through the catalogue of films playing I saw a raft of Hong Kong action films, twentysomething angst, retro noir, Tarantino-inspired crime thrillers and lots of casual drug dealing and drug usage, leaving me seriously wondering how our dysfunctional family drama ever got in.

Film festivals always look for the best films they can find to play in their festivals that will pull in paying audiences.

This started me thinking about taking a stab at another no-budget feature and shaping it around what the festival screening committees look for:

- Noir, with a criminal element
- Setting it all at night, making it visually interesting
- Small, central cast
- Character-driven, with characters that are dark, loser-types
- Both overt and underlying eroticism
- Ideal festival runtime of 90 minutes or less

Nightbeats was one of the quickest scripts I've ever written. After the extremely involved *Year* script with it's 129 pages and 400 scenes, where so much wound up on the cutting room floor, I vowed to never again write anything over 85 pages. *Nightbeats* came in at 75 pages, which I figured would time out to about 85-90 minutes. The final runtime came in at 89 minutes.

I gave the first draft to Bonnie to read and an hour later she delivered her verdict:

"I love this story! It's got such an edge to it and it hooks you right from the start."

"Yeah, but I don't know if I can pull it off. And it all has to be filmed at night."

"But that's the beauty part, nobody has to take time off from their jobs. They work during the day, then meet up with us for a few hours after dark."

"But look at all the locations. We're going to have to find a club that'll let us film in and there's 25 pages of script set in this bar. This isn't going to be easy."

"So we'll find locations. I know some people and everybody likes you. This story just pulls me in. I know it's not going to be easy but this is the movie we need to do."

Bonnie was beginning to convince me, but I still saw one big obstacle:

"Okay, but what about the part of Mercy? That's a big role and it's got some tough stuff in it. She has to be able to pass for a stripper and there's some nudity required. She's a junkie. She has to look like she's doing heroin. She resorts to hooking and has the scene where she goes down on the guy. She has to be able to look like she's overdosing. And if that's not enough there's that page and a half monologue scene. That's gonna be a killer."

"I know. And you know who would be perfect for this? Lori."

The instant Bonnie suggested Lori for the part I felt a thousand watt light bulb light up in my head.

"Lori? You think she'd do it?"

"Lori could eat this part up. She'd be wonderful. It would be amazing."

"But do you think she has time for it? She lives in New York."

"So she'll take a couple weeks off work. She loves it out here in summer." Then Bonnie tapped the script in her lap. "Lori could do this part."

This was a gutsy move for Bonnie because the actor she was suggesting was her daughter. Lori majored in theatre in an east coast college and on the day of graduation she and her drama school roommates packed up their belongings and were in New York City by nightfall to begin auditioning for shows and start their restaurant careers. She had years of doing Off-and Off-Off Broadway. Several times she'd been the runner-up for a big-time part on Broadway or TV only to be edged out by an actor with a name. Finally she reached a point where she just couldn't handle another audition. Now she was married and had an eight-year-old son. We'd given her a tiny part in *Year* as a New York literary agent. It was just two small scenes but it had reignited the acting bug that she thought was out of her system, admitting to her mom, "Yeah, it was fun. It made me realize how much I missed it."

A few weeks later Lori and grandson Sam were out for one of their visits when Bonnie mentioned that we were thinking of making another movie.

"Oh yeah?" Lori said. "What's this one going to be?"

"Well, Mike's just finished a draft of the script, would you like to read it?"

"Yeah, sure." An avid reader who typically reads a novel or two during her vacation visits, Lori took the script and started in.

An hour or so later I came in from doing yard work as Lori was finishing the last page. "Wow, what a script. I love it, I really do. It hooked me right from the start. And what a great part Mercy is. Who are you going to get to do that?"

"Well," I started, glancing aside to Bonnie, "we were kind of thinking of you."

"Really?" she said, her eyes lighting up. She truly had not expected this at all.

"It's your mom's idea and I agree with her."

"We know it would mean that you'd have to be out here for a few weeks while Mike films your part," Bonnie said. "But I think you'd be wonderful."

"Wow," Lori said. "I guess I'll have to read the script again." At which point she settled back, opened the script to start studying her new lead role.

PRODUCTION:
Shooting Something For Nothing

Filming Francesca "Kitten" Natividad and Bonnie Bennett on location for *Nightbeats*.

Mike Carroll finesses a 250-watt light with diffusion material to soften the illumination on producer-actor Bonnie Bennett in a scene with actor Anthony D'Juan on the location set of *Nightbeats*.

Shooting All In One Stretch Vs. Shooting Over Time

WHEN MAKING A NO-BUDGET FILM where both actors and crew are unpaid volunteers, you have to spearhead every aspect of the production every step of the way. If someone offers to help you with props or costumes or set design or something and doesn't come through you can't blame them because there was no compensation to compel them to be there. It's your film so you ultimately have to take responsibility for everything. This is only fair since when the film makes it into festivals you will be the one who reaps all the benefits.

Finding Volunteers

Make sure the people joining you have a reason to be there, either because they want exposure to the process or they want to make films themselves and see how it's done.

Having made two feature-length D.I.Y. films and teaching classes and workshops on one-man filmmaking, I always have people asking to help out on my shoots, either for a few hours or for a couple days so they can observe and learn firsthand. It's always helpful to have an extra hand, but I never expect volunteer crew to be there every day of the shoot. For one thing, my schedules are erratic and spread out. For another, nobody's getting paid so it wouldn't be fair to expect them to be there every day.

Making Your No-Budget Feature All-At-Once

Most people I know who set out to make a no-budget feature try to shoot it all-at-once with a crew of volunteers on a two week schedule. Cast and crew use vacation time from their jobs to work ten to sixteen hour days, not to mention weekends, without pay.

To me, that's just playing "Hollywood."

You can't expect people to throw their lives up in the air when you're not paying them.

I also don't think long days are productive. Once you finish a lunch break everyone's focus shifts from doing good work to just getting done and going home.

From my own experience, by the end of the second twelve-hour day I can't think clearly anymore. I'm just keeping the camera rolling to finish and get out of there.

People talk about the heydays of Warner Brothers, Paramount, MGM and Twentieth Century-Fox, but those studios operated on a Monday through Friday, 8 to 5 work week with a very strict eye on overtime. Woody Allen and Clint Eastwood both adhere to eight-hour shooting days, sometimes less. Michael Winterbottom works five-day weeks and eight-hour straight days. Eastwood made both *Million Dollar Baby* and *Mystic River* on 36 day schedules and never once went into overtime.

Crews are happier and more productive when they're rested.

3 To 4 Hour Shooting Days

Most of my shoots are kept to just a few hours, three or four typically. When making a film for no money, getting people together for just a few hours or so a week keeps the actors' stress level down. In fact, they look forward to the next shoot.

The final day of shooting on *Year* was done in one of the actor's apartments from 11:30AM to 1:30PM during which we comfortably shot five or six scenes. When I got home and loaded the footage into the computer there were 97 shots. This wasn't from rushing but just not wasting time.

Year was shot from March 2004 to March 2005. There were times when we'd go three weeks or a month where actors just weren't available. The actors would be apologetic but I always politely said, "No problem, we'll get to it when your schedule lets up."

Nightbeats started shooting in late September 2007 and wrapped filming in May 2008.

Short Days—Save On Craft Services

When you shoot for a full day you have to feed your people. A friend of mine made his no-budget feature shooting full days on weekends and spent over $7,000 on meals and snacks alone.

On *Year* we had a couple long days and set up a "running buffet" where people could grab something to eat during breaks in shooting. I don't stop to take a break for myself when I'm filming.

My shoots are arranged around the actors' availability. They show up on time, know their lines, we shoot for two or three hours, then they take off. And I don't have to feed them. I'll always have a cooler full of bottled water on ice, but, like everybody these days, they usually have their own bottle with them.

In the first season of *Project Greenlight* novice director Pete Jones was getting a pep talk from Kevin Smith (*Clerks*) where Jones was told to expect to put on thirty pounds during the shoot. A perfect argument against craft services.

To the weight-conscious filmmakers out there, an added health benefit to making a film as a one-man crew is that you're never idle. By the end of my summer of shooting *Year* I had gone from 194 pounds down to 173. That alone should inspire you to make your movie without a crew.

Spend your money on the film—not the food.

The Back Door Lounge in Old Sacramento serves as the dream location for the after hours lounge in *Nightbeats.*

Locations

PLAN YOUR FILM AROUND LOCATIONS YOU DON'T HAVE TO PAY FOR. Start with your own home, then move on to include the homes of the other people involved in the film, the actors and whatever crew members or production assistants involved. Provided you have a good relationship with your place of work, try there as well.

Be respectful of people's property and the time that's going to be involved. Film crews are invasive. People. gear, lights, C-stands, cables, etc., creates a lot of clutter. Always wear a smile and be polite. Keep chatter down to a minimum and low voice levels. Other filmmakers have asked to film in my house and I always come up with an excuse to decline. It's one thing for me to tie up my house for an extended length of time but it's a whole 'nother ball of wax to have someone else and all their gear and their working pace, which always moves too slow for my liking, taking over my space.

When you film in other people's houses for more than just a few hours, when it's a matter of one or more days, return the courtesy by compensating them for the time you've taken. A hundred dollars a day is a good starting point. That will also keep you moving more efficiently because the longer you take the more comes out of your wallet.

The biggest advantage to shooting in your own home is that you don't have to drive anywhere. Eliminating travel time allows you to work longer.

Fewer locations = Less time driving = More scenes shot.

Keep Your Locations Real

I'm a big fan of director Michael Winner's 1960s British films, such as *The Jokers* and *I'll Never Forget What's 'Is Name* (on which our great friend and collaborator Michael Dryhurst was assistant director and marked the beginning of a seven picture partnership with Winner). All his films were made on real locations and he kept them authentic by changing as little as possible, leaving all the furniture, books, artwork and any other bric-a-brac in place. I love that aesthetic and his interior locations benefit from having that lived-in look about them.

Snap shots on the fridge, portraits on the walls, everybody's got pictures around the house and that's what makes a place look real. It's great natural set dressing, don't touch it. Unless you're shooting an insert close-up of one of the pictures no one's going to notice.

Commercial Locations

If a restaurant, bar or coffee shop allows you to shoot for a few hours on a quiet night or after hours, be sure to generously tip the workers. A $50 or $100 dollar tip will go a long way toward keeping people happy. And get you invited back.

Permits

You really only need a permit if you're going to block off a street or sidewalk or if you have production trucks requiring special parking. I drive a Toyota Corolla and all my gear fits in the trunk. My parking concerns are limited to keeping plenty of quarters for the meters. I just show up and start shooting. With a handheld camcorder and actors on wireless mics we blend into the scenery pretty well.

"In-Production" Means "Producing Footage"

IT'S ALWAYS AN EFFORT GETTING PEOPLE TOGETHER TO MAKE A FILM when everyone's doing it on their own time, so when we are together I make it a point to shoot as much footage as I can. Well-exposed, color-balanced footage with clean audio.

I shoot many different angles of a scene to have the flexibility to shape and reshape it in the editing. Even if it's a shot or two that I'm not sure I'm going to need, it could wind up being just the shot that makes the scene cut together. With enough takes and shots I can move lines around, delete dialogue, or completely restructure a scene or an entire movie.

Never shortchange yourself on footage. You never want to
have to go back and shoot anything a second time.

Keeping Track Of Your Shots

When I'm filming I'm always thinking of the shots and the coverage I'll
need for editing.

As a one-man crew I move pretty quickly and don't want to break the
momentum I've got going with the actors. Once I finish a shot I know
the next angle I'll need and what other shots I'll have to have to tie
everything together in order to feature the best of everyone's
performances.

At this point I'm generally not looking at the script but watching
what's happening in the viewfinder. I have a checklist in my head of
what I want, what I'm getting and what I need. Once I start shooting I
generally don't pause or stop to look at the script or the notes I've made
to myself. The emphasis is kept on keeping the camera rolling.

"Have I gotten the performance out of the actors? Have they pushed
themselves far enough? Do I believe it?" I make movies based on
performances, character and story. I never work from storyboards or
shot lists. It's all done by gut instinct, the moment, the location and the
light.

Lead By Example On The Set

Always keep in mind always that it is *your* set. You are the leader.
Everyone is there for *you*. They will follow your lead. Whether it is a
happy productive set or a never-ending purgatory is up to you. You
have to set the tone and the standard for decorum. No tempers, no
raising of voices. If something or someone isn't working out, put on a
tactful smile. Be calm, polite and assured. Always keep the ball rolling.
Nothing brings a set down faster than stagnancy or indecision. The last
thing you want is to see people looking at their watches.

SHOOTING:
Cinematography
& All That Camera Stuff

Sound assistant Dominick Bernal watches the camera framing on the monitor as director-cinematographer Mike Carroll works out a scene on location for *Year*.

Close-Up: David Harris as Nick in *Nightbeats.*

I Film In Close-Ups

THERE ARE NO IMAGES MORE POWERFUL THAN FACES AND EYES. Since no-budget filmmaking doesn't have money for sets, action scenes, special effects or other gimmicks, I tell my stories through the faces of the actors.

Early on when shooting *Year* I discovered the shots that conveyed the most realism were made using the long end of the zoom (getting back and being zoomed in). Even two-shots looked best when I was standing back and zoomed in on the two actors in telephoto together.

Using the long (telephoto) end of the zoom for composing images also improves the look of no-budget filmmaking. In *Nightbeats* we filmed in a lounge after closing hours. By filming scenes at the bar between two people and only shooting in telephoto close-ups I was able to keep the emphasis on the two actors without giving away that I only had two or three other volunteer extras strategically placed to be out of focus in the background.

The films of John Cassavetes (*Faces, Husbands, A Woman Under The Influence*) are told almost entirely through close-ups and telephoto shots.

Filming close-ups of an actor from ten or fifteen feet away and being zoomed in allows me to focus more intensely on their faces and eyes, rather than being in close on the wide end of the zoom, which shows not only the actor's face but everything else that's behind them. Close-ups shot with the long end of the zoom look more serious, whereas close-ups on the wide end look more cartoonish.

My visual style now is easily 90-95% telephoto close-ups, which makes shot selection very simple. It's also much cleaner in editing to cross-cut between telephoto close-ups.

Close-Ups, Close-Ups, Close- Edie (Bonnie Bennett) meets Mercy (Lori Foxworth), a fellow night traveler, in *Nightbeats*.

Close-Ups, Close-Ups, Close-Ups

In the late 1990s John Frankenheimer had to review a number of his 1950s live television dramas to be interviewed about them for reissue. One thing that surprised him was how much of the shows were shot using multiple varieties of close-ups to capture the intensity in the actors' faces and how compelling the dramas were because of that. It made such an impression that on Frankenheimer's next film he changed his normal shooting pattern of wide angles to shooting many more variations of close-ups.

My Close-Up Shot Coverage List

When shooting actors in a dialogue scene, my basic shooting setup is:

Telephoto 2-shots of the actors shot from either side.

TELEPHOTO OVER-THE-SHOULDER CLOSE SHOTS on each actor so that part of their shoulder, collar, hair is out of focus in the foreground.

TELEPHOTO SINGLE CLOSE-UPS on each actor with the lens zoomed in tighter and shifted over slightly.

When the different takes are edited together it looks like I had multiple cameras rolling. Many filmmakers can't believe that I don't shoot my films with multiple cameras because I have so many different setups. "How else could I shoot it? I'm a one-man filmmaker and there's only one of me."

Making A Movie—One Shot At A Time

Every single shot is an effort, whether it's a master shot of the biggest scene or the tiniest insert. A simple shot in the script that you think will only take a minute to knock off will run into complications:

INSERT CLOSE-UP: STAMP is pressed on envelope.

May involve having to:

- Move the camera around so that you can get the shot tight enough to still be in focus
- Work out the movement of the actor's hand so that it doesn't block the camera's view of the stamp being applied
- Shift the actor over because they're casting a shadow over the envelope

And half a dozen other bits of minutiae that compound to make a seemingly simple shot take five to ten minutes longer than you thought.

Everything takes more time than you think.

Handheld Vs. Tripod

I find that most no-budget indie movies shot on tripods and dollies are a poor-man's impression of trying to look "Hollywood" rather than having a look of their own. The irony is that so many major studio films are turning their backs on the glamorized Hollywood style in favor of something more spontaneous and gritty. *The Bourne Trilogy, The New World, Babel* and *21 Grams* all display extraordinary handheld work and natural lighting, conveying an edginess and authenticity.

You can move a lot faster with the camera on your shoulder than when you're lugging around a tripod and having to adjust it to get the right composition for every shot. Shooting with a dolly requires longer setup times, someone to push the dolly and coordination between the movements of camera and actors, taking up valuable time.

Method Acting—Method Camera

Just as actors do "Method Acting" I film with a "Method Camera." I shoot handheld so I can be fluid and adjust the camera to the actors. I don't want to limit where they can go in a scene. I work intuitively, going with the moment, responding to what's happening in the viewfinder. The scene can be completely pre-visualized in my head and be detailed shot-for-shot in the script, but once we start shooting I let the scene take over and I go with it.

Following Somebody Makes It Smoother

If your actor is moving and you're handheld it's going to be a little bouncy, but the audience's eye will be following the actor. Match your footsteps with the footsteps of the actor so that when they take a step forward on their left foot and their head rises up you're matching your movement to the rhythm of their walk, making it a movement that the eye absorbs, looking smooth and natural.

Filming an establishing shot of a building handheld will look shaky unless you see someone walking by or a car driving past to absorb some of the motion of the camera.

First Shot Of The Day—"Where do I start?"

There's so much to do on a shooting day: getting to the location, unloading gear, setting up lights, greeting everybody, figuring out the staging of the first scene. Finally, the actors are ready and warmed up, you need to start shooting except your mind is a blank. You need to get the camera rolling, but you aren't sure what the first shot is. Everybody's ready to start, you feel their eyes on you and the clock is ticking.

Richard Lester (*A Hard Day's Night, Help!*) always liked to start the day with a quick one-take shot of an actor coming down a street or going up the front steps of a townhouse that he could knock out in a few minutes while people were still arriving and getting coffee from craft services. He found it helped create a sense of momentum on the set, that the wheels were in motion. Once Lester had that first shot under his belt, the rest of the day went like clockwork.

Everyone has his or her own way of working. You can only discover yours once you start doing it.

Never Playback After A Take

I never playback a take after shooting it. It brings the set to a standstill. Everyone wants to crowd around to watch over your shoulder and the momentum of the scene is lost. As I am the director and the cameraman I'm watching everything in the viewfinder. If there's any question or doubt about a take it's much faster just to shoot another one and keep the momentum going.

Also, when shooting on tape, playing back a take in the camera runs the risk of wrinkling the tape and ruining the footage.

Turn Off The Red Tally

I don't like people to always know when I'm rolling. This especially holds true when I'm shooting a documentary. I also find the glowing red tally light on the front of the camera to be distracting. No matter what I'm shooting I always have the tally light turned off.

This can also save you some grief when shooting Guerilla-style on the streets should someone ask, "Were you filming me?" You can "innocently" claim you were just doing a walkthrough.

Insert Shots—Catching Them On-The-Fly

When shooting standard insert shots, such as:

> INSERT CLOSE-UP—DOOR KNOB
> A HAND reaches INTO FRAME and turns knob.

These are typically grabbed after a scene's been shot, the camera frames up on the door knob and an actor is told, "Okay, now just open the door." Chances are they're not going to open the door in the same pace as they did in the scene. It may match technically but it doesn't always match dramatically.

One thing I do near the end of shooting a scene is shoot one extra take with the camera zoomed in tight to pick up my insert close-ups and any other different detail close-ups to help give added emphasis for later in the editing. I may notice an actor doing some nervous bit with their hands, either consciously or unconsciously, fidgeting with their fingers or running a hand through their hair. In this last take I'll get a super-tight shot just following their hand as the actor raises it up and runs it through their hair, scratches their forehead, then brings it back down again. I may then swing the camera over and pick up the other actor picking up a cup of coffee and sipping it or doing some kind of eye movement.

These little touches that put added emphasis on ordinary things can lend a little extra detail to the performances or the scene. Tight close-ups and insert close-ups can also be lifesavers when a scene is running on too long and I need a tight close-up cutaway or two to bridge some shots together seamlessly.

Don't Use The Camera's Built-In Image Stabilizer

As much as I love the look of handheld camera, I hate shaky shots. Some people try to counter this by using the image stabilizer, which digitally blends images together to make them smoother. The drawback to this is if the camera moves suddenly or something rushes through the shot, this frame blending can cause the image to blur. At a festival when this is projected onto a screen twenty or thirty feet wide, or on a big screen TV at home, this can really stand out.

SOLUTION: Go into the camera's menu settings and set the image stabilizer to "Off." Your images will be sharper because you'll be using the full clarity of what the camera is capable of. It also means you've got to hold the camera a lot steadier.

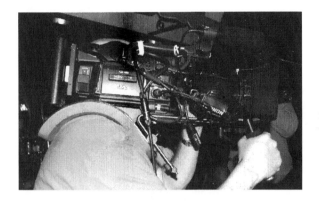

The JVC GY HD110U mounted on the Image 2000 shoulder support on *Nightbeats.*

Steady Up Handheld Shooting With A Camera Support

I wanted my films to look different from all the other camcorder movies, which are typically shot from waist-level because the operator is looking down at the flip-out screen.

Year and *Nightbeats* were both shot entirely handheld using an Image 2000[5] shoulder-mounted camera support. This consists of a curved shoulder pad with an arm extending out to a pistol grip where the camera is mounted, allowing filming using either the camera's eye piece or the flip-out screen.

Handheld camera has always looked alive and liberating to me. As a kid watching movies in the 60's I started noticing handheld camera creeping into films in fight scenes, but in European cinema handheld camera was being used much more extensively. In Richard Lester's *A Hard Day's Night* handheld shooting was demanded because of the run-and-gun schedule. Stanley Kubrick's handheld camera added newsreel-like reality to the combat and B-52 scenes in *Dr. Strangelove.*

---

5 birnsandsawyer.com or bhphotovideo.com for $295 and on Ebay for as little as $100.

Then there was the gritty in-the-streets camerawork of William Friedkin's *The French Connection* in the 70s. I'd watch these films and think, "Why can't a whole movie look like this?"

These were all filmed from the eye-level of a standing adult because they were shot with the Arriflex IIC, which had a fixed eyepiece that could not be turned up or down. To get a ground-level shot the cameraman had to lie down on the ground to squint through the viewfinder.

Another aspect to the unique look of those films is that the filmmakers themselves, Richard Lester and Stanley Kubrick, were often shooting their own handheld cameras, giving them the freedom to improvise visually and go with the action because they didn't have to whisper instructions into a camera operator's ear.

There are quite a number of other shoulder mounts that have come out since the Image 2000, some with attachments for additional camera batteries or wireless microphones, all worthy considerations. Get the camcorder out of those shaky hands and onto a steady support system.

Eliminate the middleman—operate your own camera.

Filming the wake-up scene from the end of the deathwatch sequence in *Year*. One of the rare moments when the Panasonic DVX 100A was shot handheld without the shoulder mount. The actors were so relaxed that most of them weren't acting like they were sleeping but had actually fallen to sleep.

Camcorders & Long-Life Batteries

Camcorders come with a battery included, but it's usually small and only holds a short charge. This was true of my first camcorder, the Sony TRV900, which came with a battery that could hold a charge for about an hour, as well as my third camcorder, the JVC GY HD110U, with a battery that would last for all of ten minutes.

When we headed to New York to make *Dog Soldiers* I knew I'd be out for hours at a time so I invested in a long-life battery that could run for twelve hours fully charged. I also picked up an AC power supply that could run off a cigarette lighter for recharging in a car.

The last thing you want is to be stuck on a shoot with dead batteries.

Filming Katherine Pappa in *Year* on a brutal summer day in Sacramento. When working in harsh sunlight, shoot in telephoto close-ups and shoot into the shadows.

Shooting in Daylight

IN WRITER-DIRECTOR RICHARD BROOKS' CLASSIC WESTERN *The Professionals* Robert Ryan says, "I hate the desert. It has no pity." That's how I feel about shooting in brutal overhead summertime sunlight.

Sacramento is in the northern tip of California's Central Valley, a desert climate where in the summer months the clouds stop at the mountains leaving us to be microwaved in unfiltered blue light that broils into the outer layers of your skin. The contrast ratios between what's in the shade to what's in the sun can be four to six f-stops, producing extremely harsh images. I want my images to be beautiful so these are challenging conditions.

Schedule Outdoor Shooting To The Time Of Day

For days before an outside shoot I'll study the late afternoon light, the angle of the sun and the shadows, making notes of where they are at different times of day. Then I'll schedule to shoot at specific times when I can keep the sunlight behind the actors or when the sun is low behind the treetops and off the actors entirely. Shooting at the end of the afternoon and taking advantage of the shade from rooftops and buildings, the shadows will provide a softer, more even look.

I keep the shots framed tight to exclude as much bright background as possible, isolating the actors in the shaded areas. The zoom lens is a lifesaver for this.

> If you're stuck with a cloudless day, use a tree branch in the foreground to block out as much of the sky at the top of the frame as possible.

The Lure Of Winter Light

Fall and winter light is ideal. Ingmar Bergman and his cinematographer Sven Nykvist always shot their films in the fall when the sun is lower in the sky and the angle of light is much more slanted. There's humidity in the air to diffuse the harsh light making it slightly less contrasty. Clouds in the sky soften the deadening blue light. You can be lucky sometimes and get an overcast day with beautiful soft light, free from any shadows whatsoever, allowing you to point the camera in any direction and have nice light on your actors.

Tools Of The Trade

C-Stands

ONE OF THE BASICS OF FILM PRODUCTION. Like laundry and clothespins, y'gotta have 'em.

Thin aluminum light stands can blow over in the faintest breeze, whereas C-stands are made of heavy-duty steel pipe that extend upwards six feet or so. A must when using weighty lights like an Arri 1K or the Chimera Birdcage.

Always drape a twenty or thirty pound sand bag over one of the C-stand legs to anchor it. Every time the wind blows a light over you can count on the bulb's delicate filament shattering and you can say goodbye to another thirty to forty dollars for a replacement.

Even when filming indoors weigh down a C-stand with a sandbag. If a stand gets bumped or keels over due to improper weight balance it can damage a wall or furniture. Show respect by how responsibly you use equipment in borrowed spaces.

Setting up an Arri 1K on a C-stand. Scrim is fixed across the front of the barn doors to soften the harsh intensity of the thousand watt bulb. The small black box just below his hands is a dimmer to reduce the brightness of the lamp. In foreground is another C-stand supporting a Chimera Birdcage light. Note also the orange road cones always used at night.

C-stands and sandbags can be found at higher-end camera and theatrical supply stores and B&H Photo Video (bhphotovideo.com). Craigslist is also a good place to pick up used gear at a fraction of the cost from production companies and cinematographers thinning out or liquidating.

Arri 1K

You need a strong light for illuminating large areas at night. For *Nightbeats* my key light was an Arri 1K, manufactured by Arriflex, with barn doors to clip white scrim onto and make the 1,000-watt light softer.

China Ball Lanterns—Chinese lanterns

Cinematographers like these for faces because they put out soft pools of light. For filming in a room that already has existing light of its own a China light or two is perfect to punch up the light on the actors' faces. A China light placed above the middle of a table can subtly enhance candlelight for dinner scenes. They also make terrific backlights and hair lights and are especially nice for romantic comedies.

These are nothing more than simple Chinese paper lanterns you can pick up for five bucks at stores like IKEA. Put a 500W photoflood inside with a dimmer and you're good to go. Or you can invest in JEM Ball lights (jemlighting.com), starting around $1500; a staple item on most Hollywood sets.

Chimera Birdcage Lantern Light

I was considering a JEM Ball light when Chimera (chimeralighting.com) introduced the Birdcage lantern for only $400.

The Birdcage lantern consists of two flat 8.5" aluminum disks extended from each other by 14" metal posts with a 500W light socket inside. Around this is wrapped white diffusion material that puts out a beautiful soft glow. It also comes with black masking material that wraps around a portion of the white fabric like barn doors to limit the field of light.

The Birdcage comes with a light socket adapter so you can use a basic $8 photoflood or you can use a specialty lamp designed for the Birdcage that runs around $40 per bulb. I started *Nightbeats* with the basic $8 photoflood with the intent of switching to the specialty lamp when the photoflood burned out. Eight months later when the shoot wrapped the original $8 bulb was still working.

> SIDE NOTE: The diffusion material wrapping around the Birdcage is also good at keeping insects away from the light at night. Nothing smells worse than a burning bug and they're hard to scrape off your light the next day.

Filming the deathwatch sequence in *Year*. Broadcast monitor on a rolling C-stand

is facing away from camera to aid sound assistant Dominick Bernal to know where to hold the boom mic so that's out of frame.

Monitors—See Everything Your Camera Does

Year was shot with the Panasonic DVX100A. It's not uncommon on camcorders for 3%-5% of the edges of the frame to be cropped out of the viewfinder and the flip-out screen. I needed to see exactly what my camera was getting. I didn't want to be screening in a festival and suddenly see a mic boom drop into the top of the picture.

I bought a small seven-inch portable broadcast monitor that could run on a battery, very useful when filming on remote locations. The advantage to a broadcast monitor is that you can punch a button and see a true 100% of the picture coming out of the camera.

Dominick running the boom on the death watch sequence in *Year*. The small mic at the end of the boom is an inexpensive $120 Oktava that was incredible for recording clean sound indoors.

Rolling C-Stand—Keep The Monitor Close

Most people set monitors up on top of C-stands because they're rock solid. However, when you change camera angles it requires removing the monitor, moving the C-stand to the next position and reattaching the monitor. A lot of hassle.

Since I handle so many jobs on the set I got a C-stand with a lockable wheel base so I could easily roll the monitor around with me with one hand while handholding the camera with the other.

On the times when Dominick Bernal was with me as soundman he could always see exactly what I was shooting so he knew just how close he could have his shotgun mic above the actors' heads to keep it out of frame.

Having a portable monitor on a wheeled stand was invaluable. I was concerned that many of the fine points of the actors' work could escape me by only having the Panasonic's 2-inch flip out screen to work from. Using a monitor that was several times larger was like watching "live rushes." In fact, I almost completely stopped using the viewfinder. I'd shoot handheld with the Panasonic on my shoulder and my eyes on the monitor just a foot or so away.

> WARNING: Do not move the C-stand and monitor together. They are heavy and you can easily knock something over.

Shooting Telephoto—Eliminating "Signage"

I rarely shoot wide angles on urban streets because it's almost impossible to avoid store names, ads in windows, billboards, posters on walls, etc. One of the first things a distributor will want to know is if your paperwork is in order, meaning photo releases and clearances.

Aside from the fact that I prefer the look of telephoto footage shot with a wide open f-stop to have the background out of focus, it serves the dual purpose of blurring out any readable or recognizable brand names, or "signage," behind the actors.

When setting up a shot on a street I carefully scan the area for "signage" and adjust my framing to keep them out of view, adapting my filmmaking to the surroundings. Should an actor walk past a storefront with product ads in the windows I'll shift the camera to frame them out.

If you're shooting a romantic comedy in a bar with a big neon Bud Light sign glowing behind your couple and there's nothing offensive about the scene Anheuser-Busch might be cool with you. On the other hand, if your scene's about a lying, stealing, cheating, alcoholic pedophile you may have problems.

Shooting *Nightbeats* in a real bar I was always watchful for background "signage." I never moved anything for fear of breaking something. Instead I carefully shot around these signs using the telephoto end of the zoom and framing the actors in close-ups. This also helped to make my four or five extras look like many more by constantly rearranging them in the background.

Details, details, details. Filmmaking is all about the details.

Handheld Telephoto—Controlling Action In The Background

In addition to keeping "signage" out of the background of the shots I also don't like seeing people not associated with the film in the background. I feel it distracts the audience's eyes from the actors. During a take if someone happens to walk into the background of a shot I will shift the camera to frame them out.

Camera Slates—A Waste Of Time

In *Power*, the short film I D.P.'d for Michael Dryhurst, there was a party scene where there were so many angles necessary to cover the scene that we thought it might be speedier to shoot with two cameras, locking the A-camera down on a tripod in a medium shot while I operated the B-camera for close-ups, using a slate to synch the two cameras up for sound.

Once we were rolling our designated "clapper" put the slate within a few inches of the actor's faces and snapped it down with a crack so sharp that it made the actors blink. After two attempts at this Michael and I looked at each other and mutually agreed it wasn't working and returned to our single-camera.

Using a glidecam to get the powerful Sony TRV900 in close on Carol Miranda as writer-producer-director Michael Dryhurst watches the action on the flip out screen.

Ever since I've viewed slates as distracting and rude. In today's filmmaking slates can be done electronically and soundlessly. Using a slate when recording sound directly into the camera is nothing more than "playing Hollywood."

> DSLR cameras can be a exceptions to this, of course. But even then, if there is a decent on-camera mic to record a reference track and actors are being recorded through wireless mic's feeding into a digital audio recorder, there is ample software available that will synchronize the sound based on the audio waveforms. Unless the sound you are trying to record is too far beyond the on-camera microphone's range, snapping a clapper board at the top of every take is not necessary.

Slates—Synching Two Cameras

Slates are, however, the simplest solution if you're shooting with two or more cameras. In this case all the sound is typically recorded in the A-camera and the B-camera is only shooting picture and natural sound for synching. Both cameras roll on a single slate in order to marry the B-camera with the A-camera's sound.

I served as D.P. on a one-day shoot for *Rachel*, a short film for filmmaker Chris King (watermarkfilms.net) who wanted to make a film in the Michael Winterbottom-*Wonderland* method, meaning two cameras (in this case Panasonic DVX100 camcorders), natural light and wireless mics. This was my first two-camera shoot where we also had a soundman, my neighbor Jimmy Bell.

As I abhor the loud snap of a camera slate I decided to do tail slates where the cameras are slated at the end of a scene rather than the beginning. Of course, at the end of the scene Chris called "Cut" and we both stopped our cameras without ever doing a slate. Fortunately, there wasn't any dialogue in the first two takes so it didn't matter. After that I resigned myself to slating the old-fashioned way at the start of the scene. However, we snapped the slate off to the side and away from the actors, then swung our cameras around and framed up to begin shooting the scene.

Filming *Rachel*—soundman Jimmy Bell, Mike Carroll on camera, writer-director Chris King.

Digital Camcorders & Depth Of Field

Because of the close proximity of the rear element of lenses in digital camcorders to CCD sensors there is a very deep depth of field, meaning virtually everything is in focus.

In motion pictures shot with traditional 35mm film cameras the rear element of the lens is further from the film it is exposing, producing the exact opposite effect of having very shallow depth of field. The advantage to this is best noticed in close-ups of actors where the faces will be tack sharp and the background is soft and out of focus. This separates the actor from the background and directs the audience's attention to the perfectly focused face.

With a digital camcorder you can be zoomed in on an actor's face, but if you're filming outside on a sunny day the actor's face and almost everything else will be in focus as well.

Screw-On Neutral Density Filters

The built-in neutral density filters in camcorders are just barely enough to get by when shooting in bright sunlight and you're still stuck with that depth of field problem of everything being in crisp focus.

Lately I've returned to the old tried-and-true solution from my 35mm Nikon days: an ND3 (Neutral Density) screw-on filter. The ND3 is the darkest of the neutral density filters and works like putting a pair of super-dark sun glasses over the lens. It doesn't alter the color but just cuts down on the amount of light coming in through the lens. An ND3 is the equivalent of cutting down on three or four f-stops.

For example, on a bright, sunny day I would have to stop my lens down to f-16 or f-22, making everything tack-sharp. By screwing on an ND3 filter the light would be reduced to f-4 or f-5.6, greatly softening the background. If I'm shooting a close-up of an actor using the telephoto end of the zoom the actor will be nicely focused with whatever is behind them nice soft blur.

Protect The Camera's Lens With A UV Filter

An Ultraviolet filter is a clear glass filter and will not effect the color, the focus or the exposure, but it will protect your lens from getting scratched. Once your lens has a scratch on the front element it's very costly to get fixed. On the average camcorder, where the lens is built into the camera, it can mean having to replace the entire zoom lens at a cost of several hundred dollars or more. When I order a new camera I also order a matching UV filter and screw it on over the front of the camera lens to protect it as soon as I unpack the camera out of the box.

Matte Boxes & Neutral Density Gel

Another handy tool is a matte box. When shooting *Year* I was constantly battling light reflections that produce little circles of flare into the lens. I was always having to hold my hand over the top of the Panasonic DVX 100A's lens to block out unwanted light from showing up in my shots.

For *Nightbeats* so much of the shooting was being done on streets at night, which meant that every light, street light and headlight would be a potential problem, so I invested in a matte box.

A matte box fits onto the front of the camera and has top and side panels for blocking light from the camera lens. It also has slots for dropping in square glass or resin filters, most commonly 4x4" in size.

Matte boxes aren't cheap, but nothing in filmmaking is. Depending on the brand and how involved you want to get you can spend from

$500 to $3,500. I found mine on eBay for $175.

D.I.Y. ND3 Or ND6 Filters For Just $4

I picked up some scrim and colored gels from a lighting supply for my lighting kit for *Nightbeats,* and also picked up an 18x24" neutral density gel for $4.

I cut out two 4" squares, slid them into the filter slot on the matte box and put a piece of tape over the top to keep the wind from blowing them out. I could then go into the brightest sunlight and film with the f-stop wide open, allowing me to completely isolate my subject(s) by throwing the foregrounds and backgrounds completely out of focus. I showed some test footage of this to a cinematographer friend whose first reaction was, "Did you shoot this with an Aaton or an Arriflex?"

Shoot Your Film "Clean"

If you shoot your film in a stylized way with filters you'll be stuck if it doesn't work. The best cameramen shoot good, clean, well-exposed footage.

With Final Cut Pro, Adobe Premier, After Effects and Magic Bullet you can achieve almost any look you want.

Most films released in black-and-white are shot in color. If black-and-white doesn't work, they're still able to be released in color.

It's important to have a vision, but don't burn your bridges.

Boosting the Gain

Gain works fine in digital filmmaking. Don't be afraid of it. You can easily boost your video to +6db when shooting in low light. My night footage is always shot on +6db, and occasionally on +12db, with imperceptible results. On night scenes you can get away with extra grain. Audiences have grown accustomed to grain from movies where D.P.'s use faster speed film (ASA 500) to shoot in lower light and still get detail in the shadows. On top of that, almost everybody's got a camcorder nowadays and people have become more accepting of lower quality images.

I wouldn't recommend going to +18db unless you're doing a documentary where the last thing you want to do is to put on a light.

White Balance

All camcorders have an automatic white balance or "preset." Each camcorder works differently, some better than others. The look, texture and color tones have a lot to do with the camera's manufacturer.

For the first six months that I had the Sony TRV900 I shot everything on auto-white balance. Then I started noticing that when shooting in direct sunlight things looked slightly bluish and people's skin tones had a cold, metallic feel. I switched to a manual setting to select a warmer, slightly golden feel.

Become familiar with your camcorder, test it in all types of light conditions.

TV Cameraman's Trick—White Balance In The Shade

You don't have to have a perfect white card to get a white balance. Shoes, socks, T-shirts, underwear, cars, walls anything white will do.

If you balance off something white in bright sunlight it will look fine *only* as long as you're shooting in sunshine. Once you turn to shoot into the shade of a tree or a building you'll need to white balance again or it will have a bluish tint.

I like warmer tones so I'll balance off something white in the shade, which gives the picture a warmer tone. It also means I can shoot in any direction, in bright daylight or in shaded areas, and won't have to worry about that bluish tint in the shade.

This is especially handy for documentary filming where things can be happening quickly in varying light conditions.

Panasonic DVX100A & White Balancing On Faded Levi's

When I first started shooting *Year* with the Panasonic DVX100A in 24p I could not get a good white balance to save my life. So I tried getting a balance off other colors, zooming in on yellows, reds, greens, but everything was coming out cold and austere, like a stainless steel autopsy table. Out of desperation I finally aimed the camera down at the knee of my faded blue jeans, pressed the white balance button and suddenly everything looked great. Skin tones were rich and warm, exactly the look I wanted. From that moment on whenever I was filming I always wore faded blue jeans or kept a pair in my camera bag.

The Magic Of "Preset"

On *Nightbeats*, shot on the JVC GY HD110U, straight out of the box I white balanced and the color looked great, but once we started shooting downtown at night I couldn't get a white balance. Just as on *Year*, I tried balancing on whites in light, on whites in shadows, on yellows, reds, my faded blue jeans. Whatever the camera whited on under artificial lighting came out blue and cold. I was near wit's end when I inadvertently bumped one of the camera buttons to "Preset" and suddenly everything was right with the world. After all my efforts to capture a white balance, all I had to do was set the camera on automatic and do nothing. From that evening on through the next eight months of shooting I never bothered to white balance again. I left the camera on "Preset" and JVC took care of me.

Every camera model and manufacturer is different. Never rule anything out. The only rule is to make it look good.

Edie (Bonnie Bennett) sings at the all-nite lounge in *Nightbeats.* Using shadows to create mood.

Lighting

I hate lighting.

I can't stand watching a movie and knowing where the lights are set up. I prefer "source lighting," lighting that looks like it's coming from actual fixtures and doesn't look like it's been lit. If I can't believe the lighting then it's hard to believe anything else. I want images that are natural, believable and honest. Nothing contrived or false.

I typically don't use more than two lights. I never want a face fully lit. The key light is set up on the far side of the actor(s) so that I'm shooting into the more shadowed side of the face. To me, lighting is painting with shadows, the way people look in a real place where the lighting isn't perfect. If the source light is coming from off to the side and just slightly behind them, I find that beautiful.

Over-Lighting = Phony Lighting

I try to shoot quickly and as simply as possible, adopting the Michael Winterbottom-*Wonderland* method of handheld camera, natural lighting and wireless microphones. There's an authenticity to this style of filmmaking.

I hate phony night scenes where every actor has a key light and a hair light and there's diagonal blue light on a wall that's supposed to represent moonlight, and maybe a veil of blue-lit mist at the end of a wetted-down street. I've *never* seen a glowing azure mist on a street at night.

There are websites where aspiring cinematographers post their audition reels that drive me crazy because everybody's work is exactly the same. They've all got slashes of blue light to tell us it's nighttime, they've all got the same dolly moves, and they're all composed just a little too loose to be involving. In short, their effort to look "mainstream" or "professional" only comes across as cliché.

Sydney (Christine Nicholson) and Miles (Eric Wheeler) enjoying a lazy morning in bed in *Year*. Created with a single 500 watt light raised high in a corner with barn doors and scrim. The composition is an homage to Francois Truffaut's *Bed And Bored*.

Light The Room, Not The Actor—The "European" Method

Starting in the 1960s the great European cinematographers Sven Nykvist and Raoul Coutard started putting silk diffusion or tracing paper over windows and shooting strong light in, creating soft, even, natural-looking light. This allowed the camera to be placed anywhere in the room and able to shoot in any direction, extremely helpful when working on a tight schedule.

Ava (Bonnie Bennett) and Miles (Eric Wheeler) have iced tea in her kitchen in a completely naturally lit scene in *Year*.

Making The Light That's There Work For You

There's a scene in *Year* where Miles (Eric Wheeler) pays a visit to Ava (Bonnie Bennett) at her house. She invites him in, they have iced tea, and he gives her some pictures left behind when his former girlfriend, Ava's younger sister, abruptly moved out.

Rather than set up lights I took advantage of the soft light coming in through the kitchen windows. I never shot towards the windows, which would have cast Eric and Bonnie as silhouettes, though that would have looked nice too. Instead I shot across Eric and Bonnie to take advantage of the soft, natural light filtering in from outside. This was part of my approach to shooting *Year* in a documentary style and not to light if I could help it.

Nick (David Harris) and Mercy (Lori Foxworth) reflect on their lives in *Nightbeats*. Lighting the far sides of the faces and backs of heads to bring out the shadows of the night.

Lighting The Night On *Nightbeats*

MY SECOND FEATURE *NIGHTBEATS* IS A NOIR set in the world that exists after midnight so almost every scene had to be lit or have augmented lighting. Never having taken a course or read a book on lighting I had to teach myself how to light the night without making it look like it was lit at all. I decided to make the night exterior scenes look as if they were lit from street lamps or building security lights.

To achieve this I used just two lights set far apart in a cross-lighting pattern and boosted the JVC GY HD110U camera to +6db to get better shadow detail. I also kept the lighting from looking too perfect. A rough story needs a rough edge.

Find Locations That Have Their Own Light

Throughout *Nightbeats* there are a number of recurring scenes of one of the main characters, Dubois (Anthony D'Juan), walking the city streets. These were all filmed over a few hours on a single night using only existing street light. Anthony and I met up one evening as soon as it was dark and just drove around downtown looking for locations that had interesting lighting from street lights, light spilling out from storefront windows and from parking garages.Then we'd pull over, I'd set the camera up on a tripod (one of the rare times a tripod was used) and I'd film Anthony from across the street with traffic passing in the foreground, with a metro rail train passing in the distance, whatever looked good with the light that was there. Some scenes were scripted and others we made up because the location was interesting. As it was just Anthony and me, we were able to shoot quite a number of scenes in just a few hours.

Lighting Without AC Power—High-Powered Flashlights

There were a couple shots I needed of Lori as Mercy on the streets where there was no way I'd be able to get AC power, but needed just a touch of accent lighting on her face.

I went to Home Depot and bought two high-powered flashlights that put out million watt beams of light and bounced these off a sheet of white foam core. They only lasted ten minutes on a full charge so I had two and used them sparingly.

Mercy (Lori Foxworth) contemplates her life at the beginning of *Nightbeats*. The background is lit by street lamps. Lori's face is augmented by light from a high-power flashlight bounced off a white card.

One of the film's opening shots is of Lori sitting on a bench that needed just a touch of rim lighting on her face. I filmed her in telephoto close-up from about 40 feet away, on another of my rare tripod shots, while soundman Jimmy Bell was on the other side of Lori with one of these high-powered flashlights bouncing off the white foam card to make her look naturally illuminated by street lamps.

The Power Of Reflective Road Cones

When shooting anything at night or day around any kind of traffic, cars or people, I cannot over-stress the power that orange reflective road cones wield.

When filming *Nightbeats* I put road cones next to my lights and around the perimeter of the shooting area.

One Saturday night a carload of drunk college kids drove by making catcalls at Lori in her hooker outfit. Then one of the guys yelled out to the driver, "Hey, man, look out for the cone!" The car swerved around the road cones and continued on its way.

Everybody respects a road cone. Even police will drive around them.

My Production Gear Bag: Basic Shooting Essentials

WHEN MAKING A FILM THE TRUNK OF MY CAR GETS HEAVIER for a few months: two or three C-stands, sandbags, lights with dimmers for each, hundreds of feet of electrical extension cords. And the all-important Port-A-Brace gear bag containing:

Shotgun Microphone

I've used Sennheiser ME-80 and MKH 416 shotguns, but now prefer the specificity of the Sennheiser MKH 816. *(More about this under Sound.)* When shooting a scene that has no dialogue I'll use a shotgun mic to pick up natural (ambient) sound.

XLR Audio Cables

Three, six, ten, twenty, fifty foot audio cables. Can never have too many audio cables. There are few things more frustrating than needing a cable quickly and finding all your cables knotted up. My cables are all kept coiled up in individual sandwich bags, shorter cables in small bags, long cables in gallon-size bags.

Sandwich Bags

Literally just sandwich bags from the supermarket. I store almost everything in these:

> AA batteries
> 9 volt batteries
> microphones
> wireless transmitters and receivers
> note pads
> adapters
> clothes pins

Sandwich bags are clear so you can see what's inside and keep everything clean and dry. On locations dirt, dust and damp are always issues. Resealable plastic sandwich bags are an easy low-cost solution.

Gaffers Tape—Not To Be Confused With Duct Tape

A lot of people make the mistake of buying ordinary duct tape because it's cheaper. Don't. Duct tape leaves an adhesive residue that's hard to remove and can peal off paint and wallpaper.

Gaffers tape has a cloth backing and runs around $15-$20 a roll. It can also take off paint if not used properly, so be careful. It can also save you when taping a mic to the inside of an actor's clothes.

Sony ECM 50 Lavelier Microphone

I've been using the same Sony lav mic in TV news for 25 years. These last forever and are built like a Russian tank.

In dialogue situations where the actors are stationary I'll use Sony ECM 50 mics with long cables (called "hardline," an industry term for XLR audio cables) back to the camera. The sound is clean and dependable with no frequency dropouts that can sometimes happen with wireless mics. Always have at least one on hand in the event a wireless mic acts up.

Wooden Clothes Pins

Always keep plenty of plain, ordinary wooden clothes pins on hand for clipping gels and scrim to the barn doors on lights, which get hot very quickly once they're turned on. Wooden clothes pins don't conduct heat so you can make adjustments without burning your fingers while the light is on.

Heavy-Duty Gloves

These are advised for adjusting hot lights and when raising or lowering a heavy light on a C-stand where it's easy to lose grip and risk having a pole slam down on your fingers, cutting or breaking them. Gloves also keep your hands clean when coiling up cable or extension cords in dirty situations.

> NOTE: Any time there's a possibility of a crewmember being hurt or injured take the responsibility to do that task yourself.

Be Prepared—Check, Check, Check

On a shoot day every minute is precious. Get a technical glitch and your schedule goes down the toilet. The day before a shoot I prep everything:

Charge camera batteries
Pack tapes–or memory cards if tapeless
Make sure wireless mics have good 9 volt and AA batteries
Printouts of pages to be filmed
Plenty of release forms for extras
Replacement lamps for lights

Preparedness earns respect.

NIGHT IS FOR NOIR: A Night On *Nightbeats*

Nightbeats was filmed over eight months beginning in August 2007 when Bonnie's daughter Lori Foxworth came out for three weeks of night shooting for the role of "Mercy."

As soon as Lori had returned home to New York in March, after we'd given her the part of Mercy during her visit here, she enrolled in five months of pole dancing classes to get into shape to play a stripper, losing an astounding forty pounds in the process. She also researched the part by visiting strip clubs and going backstage into the dressing rooms and hanging out with the dancers. Of course, this wasn't hard for Lori as she's very attractive and went in her Mercy costume of five inch spiked hooker boots and fishnets.

Summertime in Sacramento can be withering with 100° heat and unrelenting sunlight so night is the best time to be making a movie. We were starting during the longest days of the year when the sun wouldn't be setting until 8:30 and it wouldn't be dark enough to shoot until 9:30 or later.

During the days, while we waited for the sun to go down, Lori would be curled up with her script and a pencil, jotting on the pages. I was very curious what she was scribbling so one afternoon while she was out I flipped through her script and was amazed to find it covered with notes on thoughts that would be running through Mercy's head and indications for voice inflection for her lines. Lori's dedication in taking ownership of Mercy astounded me. You don't see that level of commitment in no-budget filmmaking.

Just as Bonnie and I look to actors we know when casting, when we need a location we first look to places owned by people we know.

For *Nightbeats* we needed a number of urban locations, streets, parking lots, alleys, all of which would be shot at night, meaning the need for access to electricity.

Bonnie had been in the cast of *Six Women With Brain Death* for the first three years of its seven-year run at The Studio Theatre in downtown Sacramento and was good friends with the theater's owner Jackie Schultz. With one phone call Jackie unhesitatingly handed over a door key and we were free to film there any evening that the theatre was "dark," the theatre term for the nights when there aren't any performances.

It's a tremendous time-saver if you can find a location that can serve as not just one but *several* different locations. The big advantage to shooting around The Studio Theatre was that everywhere you turned could be another location:

> LOCATION #1 To the side of the theatre is a small parking area with an old, pocked brick wall that says character in every time-worn square inch.
> LOCATION #2 The other side of the lot is lined with a ratty, uneven and wonderfully photogenic chain link fence.
> LOCATION #3 Directly next to that is an old garage with aging corrugated metal siding that could be another place entirely.
> LOCATION #4 Twenty feet past the garage is an alley with an unleased commercial building across the way, ideal because there would be no neighbors to disrupt in the night.
> LOCATION #5 Across the street in front of the theater is an industrial warehouse. Once a nearby pub closed around one in the morning we'd have the street entirely to ourselves.
> LOCATION #6 Finally, on the far side of the theatre was a lightly traveled street with no active businesses where, after stringing a few hundred feet of extension cords, I could set up lights and quietly take the street over for another location.

Having all these locations within a half-block of each other meant that by simply moving the extension cords and lights fifty or a hundred feet one way or the other we could be in a different location without ever having to pack up and drive someplace else. This way I could stick to the schedule and maybe even get ahead.

> When selecting locations always look for access to restrooms. An especially vital consideration when working with women.

The first Sunday night at The Studio Theatre was slated to be the first of two nights of scenes with Lori and Anthony D'Juan, playing "Dubois," a writer with a deteriorating eye disease that has made him extremely sensitive to light so that he can only go out at night. In the story Dubois and Mercy meet every night for coffee before she goes to

work as an exotic dancer. The interior scenes of the cafe would be shot later in the week. On this evening we'd be using the alley and parking lot at The Studio Theatre to stand in for the locations that are supposed to be behind the cafe.

I'd already been shooting with Lori for three nights by this time, but this would be the first night of shooting any dialogue scenes with another actor. The scenes we'd be shooting would be of them walking through the alley and then some scenes around her car, representing two different nights in the script.

The following night, Monday, was set aside for shooting an eight minute scene that included a seven minute monologue. I felt it would be too much of a stretch trying to cover both this evening's scenes and the monologue all in one night. But I also let them both know ahead of time that if the evening's shooting proceeded smoothly I'd like to keep the option open of staying on and taking a crack at the monologue, which would mean shooting deep into the night. On the surface this sounded like a tall order, but one thing I've learned about actors is that when the work is going well the adrenalin kicks in and they like to keep going while the momentum is hot.

Anthony came over to the house around 7 or 7:30 while it was still light out and we did a loose dialogue rehearsal of the scenes we'd be shooting. This was the first time I was going to be hearing any of the dialogue from the script and it was going to be my only opportunity to get them into the "Zone" before we started shooting. Lori and Anthony wouldn't be doing any physical staging, just running through the lines. Remarkably, they were both in the ballpark the first time out. We did one more run-throughs to tweak things here and there and bring the overall level of their voices down a notch. This time it was very nearly there, just enough to start filming, so we packed into our cars and headed off for The Studio Theatre.

With the key Jackie had given us I let myself into the theatre, then unloaded the electrical extension cords from the Toyota's trunk, plugged them into wall sockets inside the theatre, then ran the cords

out to the parking lot and started setting up lights. The extension cables I'd picked up from Home Depot for around $200 were a variety of 50 foot and 100 foot heavy-duty waterproof cables that could withstand a car driving over them and were in bright orange and yellow colors to stand out in the dark.

Almost all of these location scenes were lit with just two lights, an Arri 1K with scrim over the barn doors for diffusion and a Chimera Birdcage light with a 500-watt photoflood. Each light was mounted on a C-stand, anchored with sandbags and marked with a reflective orange road cone. On a vary rare occasion a third light would be pulled out, a small Lowell Mini-Pro with a 250 watt bulb and scrim on the barn doors. I wouldn't be needing it on this night, though, so it stayed in the trunk of the Toyota.

The first shots were of Lori and Anthony walking through the alley; moody shots with no dialogue. The lighting here was just augmenting the parking lot and alley lights that were already there.

Not needing to worry about the sound for these first shots without dialogue was a relief because there was a restaurant with a patio right next door where a group of waiters and bartenders from another restaurant that had already closed for the night were hanging out, drinking, and peaking over the fence and making catcalls at Lori in her Mercy hooker garb. We had another scene from later in the film with Anthony as Dubois walking through the alley alone so we shot that one next while the lights were in place.

The next scenes planned for the night were to be shot just thirty feet away on the side parking lot of The Studio Theatre. The first one that we'd be shooting was the scene that came after the shots of Dubois and Mercy walking through the alley and picks up with them coming to her parked car where they have a brief exchange of dialogue. It would take twenty to thirty minutes to light and to get Lori and Anthony set up with wireless mics for sound. We figured that by the time we were ready to shoot the crowd at the restaurant would have quieted down or split. Lori and Anthony ran their lines while I moved the lights and cables.

When shooting at night I keep the light levels as low as I can to take advantage of whatever lighting already exists from street lamps, light spilling out from windows, building security lights, whatever. I just augment with enough light to illuminate the actors.

NOTE TO ONE-MAN D.P.'S & GAFFERS: Don't rush when moving lights around. When you hurry you get clumsy— drop a light and ruin it or the bulb, dent a car, break a window, or trip and hurt yourself. Also, when working with long electrical cables you need to be extra cautious.

By the time we were ready it was 10:45 and I was anxious to get going on the first dialogue scene. The ruckus from the restaurant patio had died down and we started rolling on our first take. From the start I could tell we had a good scene going. Then thirty seconds into it, once Lori and Anthony started to speak, laughter erupted from the restaurant patio. We waited a few seconds and started over. Again, as soon as we started getting into the dialogue the off-duty restaurant group would get loud. We tried a third take, the same thing. By now it was starting to seem intentional. We looked over and these drunken sods had their heads poked over the top of the fence laughing at us, then saw us looking at them and ducked down out of view.

Lori, who is a restaurant manager back in New York, went over to talk to the kids. They apologized and said they'd hold it down, but by this time we'd lost faith in them.

It was now almost eleven o'clock and all I had to show for it were a couple of walking shots. I'd spent a half hour very carefully arranging the lights for these next scenes and now I was realizing that the only way I was going to get anything from the night's shooting was to move to a quieter spot further away from the off-duty restaurant crew. Another hundred feet or so away was R Street, which ran in front of The Studio Theatre. The Irish Pub down the block was closed and the street was completely empty. Time to make a decision.

I apologized to Lori and Anthony and said the only thing to do, without staying put and pulling our hair out, was to move the setup over onto R Street. Both Lori and Anthony were as frustrated as I was and readily agreed.

I pulled out more extension cords to reach over to R Street, put cones out across the parking lot over the cables, repositioned the Toyota and set up the Arri 1K and the Chimera Birdcage in a cross-lighting pattern around the car. It was infinitely quieter here and, truth be told, once I looked through the view finder at Lori and Anthony coming around the battered chain-link fence to the car I found the visuals at this location to be much stronger.

It was approaching midnight and, finally, we were getting some real footage with dialogue and interaction between the characters of Mercy and Dubois. The lighting was working. The mics were fine. There wasn't any traffic. It was after midnight on a Sunday and the city had gone to sleep. Even the little restaurant with the patio was closing up and the waiters and bartenders were clearing out. We had literally commandeered this block-long stretch of R Street and the neighborhood belonged to us. It was time to focus on the film.

Lori and Anthony were marvelous together. I honestly can't remember saying anything to them about what to do or how to do it. They were truly in the "Zone" from the first moment.

When I shoot a scene, no matter how long or short it is, I don't break it down into a series of short bits that are strung together later in the editing room. Every time we roll I shoot a full take of the whole scene, whether it's a brief thirty seconds or runs for eight or nine minutes. We shoot the entire scene every time. At the end I might go, "Yeah, that was great. Let's try it again, only this time bring it down a little more." Then we'll quickly start over again while the actors are still warmed up and in the moment.

One finicky thing I've discovered about setting up lights is that every time the camera is shifted slightly from one side to the next requires a subtle shifting of the lights as well. So after every take I'd have to put the camera down, walk over and move a light a few feet one way or the other, weigh it down with the sandbag again, put the camera back up on my shoulder, check through the viewfinder to see if the lighting's right and go on to the next take. I felt bad that the evening was going on and on so I was constantly apologizing to Lori and Anthony, but they were both completely into the moment and unconcerned. While I was dealing with the lights they were running their lines and keeping in character. Each different angle on them never required more than one or two takes.

Once a police squad car cruised by, but never stopped. They were probably curious about what we were doing not to mention wanting to check out Lori in her hooker outfit.

We were moving now. Not fast, but steady. As I mentioned earlier, I'd scheduled two nights for shooting the Mercy and Dubois scenes and planned for us to return the next night, Monday, to shoot Mercy's seven minute monologue that tells what happened to her as a teen-ager that led her into the night world.

This was the scene that had sparked the whole film. Almost exactly a year before I was in my studio working on a completely different script when I suddenly started having a monologue start playing out in my head of a woman telling her life's story to somebody very late one night in a car. I put aside what I was working on, wrote it all down and e-mailed it to my filmmaker friend Chris King to get his reaction. He e-mailed back almost instantly saying he thought it was killer stuff and that it had the potential to be the beginning of a very interesting and haunting movie.

A monologue is the glue that holds a good theater piece together, but it can be the iceberg that sinks the ship in a movie. So a few days before the Sunday night shoot I had a rehearsal with Lori to hear the monologue to get a sense of how long it was going to play and whether I needed to cut or rewrite any of it. We went out to the studio and Lori sat on the sofa and Bonnie and I sat back in chairs to listen. She took a few seconds to get herself into the character of Mercy, then did the entire two page monologue word perfect. She was mesmerizing.

Every second of that seven-minute monologue, telling of the story of Mercy's life that she'd never revealed to anyone before, was like witnessing someone nakedly exposing their very soul. I never imagined that someone could be dedicated so intensely to a fictitious character that I'd invented. I knew right then that holding the camera in close-up on Lori's face as she told this story could transfix an audience and would be the spine that held the entire film together.

When she had finished Bonnie looked over to me and said, "Is my daughter good or what?"

It was now just after one o'clock in the morning. In spite of all our delays we'd managed to finish our night's shooting almost right on schedule. The blistering August afternoon of one hundred degree heat had now cooled to the low eighties with a soft breeze and Lori and

Anthony and I were all wide awake. The city had gone to sleep and the streets around us were dead quiet. Perfect conditions for recording great sound. If we went ahead and wrapped for the night and tried to pick up again the next evening, aside from the actors having to work themselves back into the "Zone" again, we'd be starting all over with the same sound issues or worse that we'd suffered at the start of the evening. The lights were in place and they were in the acting moment.

"Look, I know it's late, but we're doing really good right now. How would you feel about staying on and giving the monologue a shot?"

"Yeah, sure," Lori said without a second thought.

"That's what we're here for," Anthony joined in. "Let's do it. None of us are working tomorrow anyway."

The monologue scene takes place in Mercy's car with the two of them sitting in the front seats. I lowered the lights to angle in through the car windows. Just as I was about to declare the street mine two cars pulled up at the other end of the block in front of the pub. A moment later we started to hear clattering clicks and clacks. I looked around and my spirit suddenly began to sink.

"Oh, crap—skateboarders."

Lori started to get out of the car. "I'll go and talk to them."

"No, no, let me go try this time."

I strolled over to the cars, the camcorder on my shoulder, to where a couple kids on skateboards were riding the handrails and jumping off the cement steps of the closed pub.

"Hey guys."

One of the older fellows turned around. "Oh, hey, you guys shooting a movie down there?"

"Yeah, we are."

"We makin' too much sound for ya, aren't we?"

"Well, yeah, kinda."

"Yeah, I was afraid of that. No problem. We can go somewhere else."

"Thanks, that would really be a big help." I couldn't believe it would be this easy.

"Hey, is that the JVC?"

"Yeah."

"How you like it?"

"It's great. Puts out a killer picture."

"Cool. Yeah, I just got the new Panasonic."

"Yeah? Whatta you shoot with it?"

"Skateboard videos."

"Cool."

That was it. They were already loading back into their cars and taking off by the time I got back to Lori and Anthony. I suddenly had new respect for skateboarding.

During the day you can hardly find a place to park on R Street, but at two in the morning on a Sunday night in August we owned the night. The Arri 1K and Birdcage lights were in place, the Toyota was parked sideways along the street because it worked better for the camera angles, and there was no one around to tell me otherwise. I set up a folding chair in the middle of the street with an orange reflective road cone next to me to let any late-night drivers know I was there. I slouched down in the chair to film an eye-level side two-shot of Lori and Anthony in the front seats as she tells him the story of her life.

"Okay, I'm rolling. Go whenever you like."

Lori settled into her "Zone" for a second or two, then began. I'd anticipated needing the whole of Monday evening for shooting the monologue because I wasn't sure how many times we'd have to stop and start to get all the way through it. It never occurred to me that an actor would be able to go through the entire two pages in a single take without missing a line, but Lori not only did the monologue in one take, she did it perfectly.

"Wow. Okay. Don't move. I'm just gonna shift the camera over for a closer angle."

I said this very softly because I didn't want to break the level of intensity she'd brought to the scene and was still in. I moved the chair a few feet over to the side of the car to get a closer shot on her, trying not to waste any time and lose the moment she was in. As I was doing this I heard Anthony over his wireless mic say, "That . . . that was great."

I framed up on Lori and started the camera again, "Okay, Lori, I'm rolling. Whenever you want." I reinforced my arm supporting the JVC camcorder for another long take and, again, Lori delivered the monologue with the same emotional intensity—in one take.

I shifted the camera to get a single close-up on Anthony. As much as Lori had to prepare for this scene Anthony had an equally challenging task, he had to be the straight man. He had to sit, listen and react. So much of *Nightbeats* is told through Dubois' point of view. He has to take in Mercy's story with empathy, but without judgment. Dubois needs her story to fill in the puzzle pieces of the book he's writing about the night world. Just as with Lori, Anthony was right there in the moment and, just like Lori, he did it in one take.

This massive scene that had hit me in the middle of an afternoon twelve months earlier and that inspired the entire film we were now embarked on, and which I'd scheduled an entire evening for, was completed in just three single seven minute takes in less than forty-five minutes.

We shot a couple of insert close-ups of Anthony turning a digital voice recorder on and off, then he was wrapped by around 3 AM. Lori and I stayed on for another half hour filming a few detail shots of Mercy taking a hit of black-tar heroin (in this case a strip of aluminum foil smeared with marmite) and then we were wrapped.

I broke down the lights, coiled up the cables, stowed everything back in the trunk, locked up the theater and we headed home.

Once we'd gotten past the early evening's sound issues and made the move to the better location it had become a truly pleasurable night. There's something to be said for working late at night. Yes, it takes a physical toll on you, but after 1 AM everything becomes strangely settled and still and something otherworldly and magical starts to happen. And being a Sunday night made the quiet street all the quieter.

Also, the night doesn't show the passage of time the way it does during the day. You don't have to deal with the sun arcing across the sky and the constant changing of light and shadow. Instead, there's a perpetual canopy of stars above you and a sense that time is standing still. That whatever you're doing is not in a forward direction but sideways in a timeless, surreal movement of it's own.

As we were driving home I was thinking about how productive we'd been, just the three of us. How much we'd managed to shoot in a matter of only six hours without ever feeling like we were rushing or compromising. Just maintaining a smooth, steady pace. From 9:30 in the evening to 3:30 in the morning we'd completed two scheduled nights of scenes; almost nine minutes of the finished film.

I couldn't help but think of the legendary New York film director Sidney Lumet who always said, "The key to making a good scene is easy -- you just get good actors."

DIRECTING ACTORS:
Letting Them Do What They Do

Discussing an upcoming dialogue scene between Francesca "Kitten" Natividad and Bonnie Bennett in *Nightbeats*.

Directing On The Set

I COULD TELL AN ACTOR EXACTLY WHERE I WANT THEM TO STAND, what I want them to do, how to say every line and where I want their eyes to be looking. And if I ever did any of that I'd be a perfect idiot.

My first few times going over a monologue with my wife Bonnie I directed her on every inflection, every pause and emphasis on every word. She listened patiently and did everything I asked. Then afterward she explained that if I tell actors exactly how I want them to do their lines I would not have actors but marionettes and that no respectable actor would want to work with me. I never gave another detailed direction again.

When I'm shooting a scene the only people on the set are the actors and me[6] so it's important to know how to work with them.

My goal when making a film is for the actors and everyone else involved to have such a positive experience that they're jaded when working with anyone else.

I look upon making a film as making art and creating it collectively with other artists. We're creating art, not money. (At least not yet.)

Out of my respect for the actors giving me their time I try not to tell them how to do what they do. In fact, I try to say as little as possible.

---

[6] On some occasions I may have a soundman if he's available, or a production assistant who wants to see how I do things. But the vast majority of the time it's just me.

Rehearse Sparingly

I try to work with the best theatre-trained actors I can find. I figure they're experienced enough to know what to do with a part without me telling them, so I don't waste their time with lengthy read-throughs or rehearsals. Since we're making a no-budget film for the sake of art and not money I don't want to take up any more of the actors' time than needed to shoot their scenes. The most I like to do is hear the actors running their lines while I'm mic'ing them up and finessing the lighting in order to hear their approach to the dialogue and nudge them in one direction or another, if they need any direction at all, and then start shooting.

One of the best lessons I ever got in film directing was watching behind-the-scenes footage of Clint Eastwood at work. He is a revelation in simplicity. He'll casually walk through a scene with the actors then say, "Okay, let's just roll one off and see what happens. Go whenever you want." He's loathe to say, "Action," never says "Cut," and never uses video playback, standing right next to the camera and watching each take on a little wireless monitor he carries around in his hands. At the end of a take he might say, "Yeah, that was nice. Let's move over here..." One or two takes on each angle and that's it.

Another great tip was in the making-of DVD extras on Ridley Scott's *Hannibal*. Working with Anthony Hopkins, reprising his role of Hannibal Lecter, director Scott rarely said more than "A little bit more" or "A little bit less." I've adopted those simple words and been constantly amazed by the quality of results produced by this less-is-more style of directing.

When I shot the short film *Power* Michael Dryhurst brought the principal actors together on a Sunday afternoon and rehearsed a few of the longer scenes. This helped to give everybody a clear idea of their part and their relationship to one another in the story and get them all working together in the same groove. A week later when we started shooting we were able to hit the ground running.

Getting The Actors In The "Zone"

If you're going to open a film with large set-piece sequences such as a wedding, anniversary, family reunion or other event that involves all or most of your cast, don't kick off your shooting schedule with this monster. Instead, ease your people and yourself into it.

Year opens with an elaborate New Year's Eve party sequence with virtually the entire cast in the same room. The scene was filmed on Saturday, July 31, 2004, the only day I could schedule all the actors to be together at the same time and nearly four months after we'd started shooting.

I spent the Friday before covering over all the windows of our house with cardboard and hung long sheets of thick black-wrapping cloth around the front door to create a light tent blocking out every slightest glimmer of light so we could shoot the nighttime party scene during daytime hours.

Most of this sequence was shot between nine in the morning and 2:30 in the afternoon when I had to start letting my principal actors go so they'd have time to get home and rest before going on to the stage shows they were performing in that evening. We continued shooting with the fewer and fewer actors we had, finally wrapping around six o'clock. By the end of the day I had

Anthony D'Juan and David Harris run through their lines on the location set of *Nightbeats.*

over two and a half hours of footage in the can, shooting with only a single camera.

However, by the time we undertook this mammoth sequence I had already worked with all the actors for a few or several days filming smaller scenes to get them familiar with the "Zone" of performance level that I was looking for.

We started out shooting little scenes that involved only one or two actors at a time doing simple things like waking up, making coffee, talking on the phone, riding an exercise bike, working, crossing days off a calendar. Incidental scenes that didn't demand a lot of acting. All the actors had their roots in theatre where they were trained to project to the back of the auditorium, but most had little or no experience in front of a camera so I needed to acclimatize them to the naturalistic style of film acting that I was looking for.

On our first days I'd shoot lots and lots of takes. Something as mundane as getting a cup of coffee would be ten takes. The actors said my favorite phrase was, "Yeah, that was great. Let's do it one more time. And try doing it less this time."

Even on takes where I could see from the beginning that they weren't in the "Zone" I'd let them go all the way through the scene. I didn't want to interrupt by saying, "No, no, no, not like that," and run the risk of throwing off their confidence. I'd let them go all the way through to the end, then say, "That was great. Let's try it one more time and this time bring it down even more. Just relax and don't worry about the acting. Just let it go." We'd keep shooting this way until there wasn't any acting to be seen at all.

Some actors with years of stage experience develop little mannerisms. "Actorisms," I call them. Physical bits of repetitive action they've grown to rely on, such as sniffling or animated hand gestures, which needed to be wrung out.

By starting on the little scenes to get the actors into the "Zone," when the big day arrived to shoot the party sequence all the actors knew what I was looking for and the shoot went like clockwork.

Hearing Your Dialogue & Giving It Away

When I write dialogue I have rhythms in my head for how I want it to be delivered. However, as the director, I try to keep this to myself as much as possible.

The first time I hear the words spoken it's like seeing a movie that's been adapted from a book. No matter how good the movie is it's always going to be different. I have to detach myself and be open to the actors' interpretations. I have to relinquish almost everything about the parts so the actors can make them their own. Otherwise, I could ruin the chances of getting any intelligent performances.

The trick is to find good actors and then guide them in very general terms such as, "You know, I see this as being a little more tense." Or, "This is very casual. Just try playing it off the cuff."

Run-Through Up To A Point

On *Nightbeats* we wouldn't so much rehearse as we'd do a run-through. This came after I'd set up lights and the actors were mic'd and ready. I'd say, "Okay, this happens in this area. Let me just see what you have in mind, how you're seeing the scene." Then I'd stand back and watch, adjusting their audio levels on the camera as they spoke, maybe watching them through the viewfinder to find the first shot.

The fascinating thing about actors is that if you say, "Show me what you're thinking here," they won't walk casually through a scene but will start off completely in character.

"That's pretty close," I might say. "Let's look at this again and try punching this one place up a little bit more and bring it down at the end. Give me a little bit less."

Almost every time they'd start the second run-through it would be so close to what I was after that before they got too far into the scene I'd say, "Okay, okay, wait, wait, wait. This is looking too good. Let's just go ahead and roll one off."

I'd quickly get the camera up on my shoulder, frame up on them and start recording. "Okay, I'm rolling. Just go ahead and go any time you want."

Pretty much that was the extent of the rehearsing.

It Always Takes Longer To Set Up Than You Think

If you set a call time of 10AM and plan to start shooting by 10:15 don't expect to be rolling until 10:30 or 10:45.

Keep people focused between takes, particularly additional crew and extras. Don't let chatter raise the noise level so that the actors become distracted.

Allow your cast quiet time to warm up. You'd never expect a marathon runner to take off from the starting line without stretching and limbering up first. Actors have the same process.

Don't Bother Actors With Hitting Marks

I want actors to enjoy their acting and don't want to bother them with technical things like starting and stopping in specific places so they can be in focus. They've had the script, they know their lines and what their character should do, the best thing I can do is let them go. As most of my coverage is handheld close-ups the exact position of an actor isn't terribly important. I can easily adjust the camera so they can concentrate solely on their performances. Actors find this liberating and it makes them feel much less like they're on a movie set with assistants measuring tape out to their nose.

Actors + Lighting

Year was shot almost entirely with the existing lighting in the real locations we were in. As the director-cameraman I usually just said, "Let's shoot over here where the light is nice," or "That's nice light coming in over by that window, let's try it over there." By shooting in real places with the light that was there the performances tended to be more natural as well and we could move pretty quickly.

On *Nightbeats*, since we were shooting at night, *everything* had to be lit. Every shot required the Arri 1K and Chimera Birdcage lights to be positioned just so. When I shifted the camera a few feet to get a different angle the light would be different on the actors' faces, so I was constantly adjusting the lights. As a result, shoots that took two hours on *Year* became three and a half to four on *Nightbeats*. Fortunately the actors understood the time was being spent to make them look good and were patient through it all.

> **Actors work best and are happiest when the waiting is kept to a minimum and they're always kept moving.**

You Can't Force A Performance

You have to be able to recognize what your actors can do and what they either can't or won't be able to do. I may see a scene a certain way and an actor will have his or her own interpretation. Within a couple takes I can tell how close we're going to get. Some actors can only bend so far. If the actor's interpretation isn't giving me what I think the scene needs in order to work that's when I have to start reconsidering:

> **The scene isn't written well enough**
> **I'm not adequately articulating what I want**
> **The actors simply can't take the scene where I want it to go because it isn't natural**

In no-budget filmmaking you can't force performance. That only makes the actors uncomfortable and that's not helpful because you need them to keep coming back.

If I can't get the scene I want then I've got to get the best out of what the actors can give me. By shooting enough different angles and close-ups I should be able to pull something out in the editing room.

Don't Be In A Hurry To Call "Cut"

When I reach the end of a take, especially if it's a really good take, I'll keep the camera rolling a few extra seconds or so. Sometimes during a take the old term "chemistry" will kick in. There will be an unexplained electricity between the actors. It's a weird thing to explain but in the right circumstances the scene will take on a special life of its own, like having a secret portal open up and watching people in a private moment. The actors truly get inside the skin of the characters they're playing. An "Extra Inner Zone." You never know when it's going to happen or how long it will last. Sometimes it happens when the scene is over in something unscripted that they say or do; a turn, a look, you never know. You can never say, "That was great! Let's shoot another just like that." It will never be just like that again. You can't recreate magic. You may not use it but it can be interesting to see what a smart actor will do when they're handed some extra time to explore on their own.

> Respect the time people give you. Never waste it or take it for granted. Everybody has someplace they'd rather be, so use the time they're giving you wisely.

Improvising

I'm not opposed to improvising; I just don't know how to do it. The actors I use tend to come from the theatre where they have a script and make it work.

I would love to try an improvisational film. Comedy could be well suited as I feel most good comedy comes from the spur-of-the-moment as opposed to being written out, as with Larry David's HBO series *Curb Your Enthusiasm* where episodes are developed as treatments with no written dialogue and the actors inject their own sense of comedy on the spot. It would be interesting to experiment with this on a short film.

There was a small scene in *Nightbeats* involving Bonnie and Jackie Schultz playing two characters at a bar counter. In the script it was just a series of shots of the two of them talking that I planned to put music over. When we shot the scene I said, "Just go ahead and be talking about something and I'll just roll for a while." Soundman Jimmy Bell was helping me that evening so he instinctively put a boom mic on them. The incidental dialogue that Bonnie and Jackie came up with turned out to be so good that I wound up doing the exact opposite of what I'd planned and used their dialogue prominently with the music playing low under it.

> BOTTOM LINE: Don't rely on improvisation, but sometimes it can surprise you.

Morris (Michael Dryhurst) advises Ava (Bonnie Bennett) in a moment of crisis in *Year*.

Michael Dryhurst is the only actor I've worked with who's ever improvised. All the other actors, coming from theatre, stayed true to every word I wrote for them.

In *Year* there's a four-minute scene where Morris (Michael Dryhurst) visits the eldest Stone daughter, Ava (Bonnie Bennett). The scene was originally a page and a half, which Michael rewrote into seven pages. It was very good but far too long for the pace of the film so I edited it down to three pages, which was still twice as long as what I'd had in mind.

Michael embellished because he wasn't an actor and couldn't always remember the exact lines from take to take, which was fine with me. He'd been in the movie business all his life and is a great producer so playing an entertainment manager was like stepping into an old pair of comfortable shoes. If he forgot a line he'd make something up and keep going.

In one line Michael, as Morris, tells Ava of an offer from Berlin to return to the musical stage and tries to entice her with a "generous per diem." I had no idea that entertainers received per diems but Michael did and threw it in. Michael brought his life experience to the role and the scene was better for it.

I began editing the scene that evening and it took me almost two weeks to get it right. Since Michael didn't always deliver his lines the same and would frequently embellish, crosscutting the scene to play smoothly with Bonnie, who never alters so much as a comma, took some tender care. Occasionally during this Michael would drop by to see how the editing was progressing. I'm sure he was thinking of all his beautiful lines that I should have filmed. When I finished he watched the scene, smiling, and said, "Yes, it's a good scene."

In the years since I've had so many people say to me that the scenes between Bonnie and Michael are their favorites in the film.

Don't Be Married To Your Original Concepts

There's a scene in *Year* where David Harris and Kristen Elizabeth are walking along a marina in San Francisco, done in one handheld side-tracking medium close shot. I'd originally wanted to shoot this on a beach with the Golden Gate Bridge in the distance and cross-cut between them in panning telephoto shots.

The Sunday that we went to San Francisco turned out to be the warmest the city had experienced in years. The roads to the beach were jammed and trying to shoot this intimate scene amid a crowd would have been impossible. I finally settled on using a marina just a few blocks from a

Kristen Elizabeth (Lana) on location in San Francisco for *Year.*

friend's apartment where we were shooting interiors. I wired David and Kristen with radio mics that I'd been using throughout the shoot, but for some reason they wouldn't work at this location. We'd already lost an hour and a half with the efforts to get to the beach and time was ticking away. So I wired them with Sony lavelier mics hardlined to the camera and walked closely with them so the cables dangling out from the bottom of their clothes wouldn't be visible. It's not at all the sequence I had in my mind, but when I look at it now it's simple and honest and I can't think of doing it any other way.

> Always stay calm. Don't let the actors see your frustration or disappointment. Rethink and keep moving. It may not be the scene you wanted, but you can make it work in the editing and that's all the actors and the audience is going to see.

There's another scene in *Year* about a couple who've been existing in a dead marriage. In the scene the wife, Ava (Bonnie Bennett), looks at her husband Brendan (Blair Leatherwood) and says, "I can't do this anymore." I'd written a few more lines for Blair to deliver, but as we were walking through the scene Blair said, "These two people have reached an impasse where they're both beyond fighting. I don't think he needs to say anything. I think he should just look at her."

"Okay, let's play it that way," I agreed. "I'll roll and just do what you think is best."

I always try to bend to the actors' natural instincts. The scene may not play out the way I had in mind but I've found the collaboration with the actors makes it better.

When filming another scene in *Year* with Christine Nicholson as "Sidney," the neurotic sister, a couple of my lines were giving her problems. After a few takes I sensed her frustration and said, "Look, I'm sorry, I didn't write this very well. Let me rework these lines."

"No, no, no, no, it's not the lines," Christine insisted. "I can do this. I can make this work."

> Theater actors take it as a challenge to make halfway decent lines sound better than they should. Later in editing, if the lines still don't work, I can always cut them.

Working With Minors

It's a good idea to always have another adult around, and preferably a woman, when working with young girls. Over my years in news I've covered so many stories about improper conduct that I don't want anyone to ever look back and question anything on my sets.

In *Year* one of the Stone sisters, Gina, played by Katherine Pappa, has a nine-year-old daughter. In keeping with our practice of not holding casting calls, Bonnie and I asked Katherine if she knew anyone and she immediately suggested her best friend's niece, Savannah Swain. A photo of Savannah was sent to us and we sent a copy of the script to her mother Sabrina. As *Year* contains some adult themes, sexual situations, frank language and deals openly with one of the adult sisters being a lesbian, I wanted Savannah's parents to be completely aware of every aspect of the film in which their daughter would be appearing. They appreciated that I was so up front with them, read the script and gave their permission and full support.

Nine-year-old Savannah Swain, who was cast sight-unseen for the role of "Chris" in *Year*.

Year opens with a sequence introducing each of the women of the Stone family, from the grandmother to the youngest granddaughter, saying "Fuck it."

After Sabrina read the script I specifically discussed this scene to make sure that she and her husband were completely comfortable with this. Both of them understood that it was a character and saw the reasoning behind the scene and were on-board.

Savannah's scene has her stomping into her bedroom, pulling a jacket off, throwing it into a closet and saying her line. Before shooting the scene I asked Savannah, "Would you do me a favor and get your mom? I'd like her to be here when we film this." I wanted Sabrina to be present as I was directing Savannah saying this profanity.

I never said the word out loud to Savannah, referring to it only as, "And then you'll say your line." It should also be noted that Savannah and her family are very religious.

I kept the number of takes for this scene down to just a few and after each one Savannah would drop to her knees, clasp her hands to her face in prayer and apologize to Jesus. Her mother kept reassuring her that it was all right, that it was not her saying this but a part she was playing and it was fine.

At the San Francisco Independent Film Festival several people came up afterward and commented how that brief scene showed so much about that family of women and that Savannah displayed a very mature performance for such a young girl.

It Never Hurts To Ask

I always say, you never know who your friends are going to be.

A couple years ago I was out on my sidewalk holding a boom pole up in a tree recording sounds of rustling leaves for the finishing touches of *Year* when along came a guy with arms covered in tattoos and walking a dog. He went past me then turned, opening his mouth to say something -- and I already knew exactly what it was going to be: "Excuse me, what are you doing?" Instead, he said, "Excuse me, are you recording post production Foley audio?" Honest to God, those were his exact words.

Dumbfounded, I responded, "Yes, I am."

It turned out this guy, Jimmy Bell, had been living on the street directly behind me for the same number of years that Bonnie and I had our house and that he was a sound and music engineer who wanted to get into recording location sound for films.

We became instant friends. I began lending Jimmy my sound gear and referring him to people I knew for their projects. In no time he became one of the most sought after location soundmen in the city.

When Bonnie and I started planning *Nightbeats* Jimmy volunteered to run sound for me any time he was free. He also said that one of his dreams was to sound design a film.

Missy Bell as "Dancing Girl" from her parking lot striptease scene filmed on a chilly evening in October 2007.

"Hey, if you want to cut your teeth on this one," I told him, "feel free to do whatever you want."

There's a scene in *Nightbeats* where a hooker does a strip tease in a parking lot in the blazing headlights of a car. Frank Casanova, the owner of the Sacramento production facility The Studio Center (thestudiocenter.com), was letting us use the outside of his studio as a location, which has a parking area that backs up to a rail yard, so the "where" was solved. Now we had to find the "who."

One warm summer evening Bonnie and I were over at Jimmy and his wife Missy's house having wine. When Missy got up to fetch another bottle Bonnie and I saw that she had an incredible tattoo on her back. "Wouldn't that look great on the back of the stripper in the parking lot?" I whispered to Bonnie.

We delicately broached this idea to Missy, who works in internet finance, and without skipping a beat she jumped at the idea.

"You're sure?" Bon cautioned her. "You realize what we're asking you to do?"

"You kidding? I work for a bank. I never get to have any fun."

When you're shooting a film on weekends, it's all about scheduling and the availability of your actors. In this case, we weren't able to get Missy and David Harris, the actor playing the John in the car, together until the middle of October when the summer's warm nights were becoming a fast fading memory and the autumn crisp was settling in once the sun went down.

We got to the location just as it was starting to get dark. I arranged the Arri 1K and Chimera Birdcage lights around David's car and Bonnie set up an iPod with speakers to play music for Missy to dance to. Soon as it was dark we started to roll and Missy began her dance.

Missy Bell as "Dancing Girl" beginning her parking lot performance for "Nick" (David Harris), seen in the rear view mirror of his car in *Nightbeats*. An example of making the most of the lighting available. Missy is lit entirely by the headlights of David's SUV. David is lit from the side by the Chimera Birdcage light.

And she was perfect. The internet banker who had never acted before moved, enticed, played with her hair, and seductively slid her dress off to reveal her stripper bikini underneath like a natural actor playing a role.

Then we got to the tricky part.

"Uh... Mike... How do you want me to do this?"

"Well, how comfortable do you feel?"

Missy took a breath. "I need more wine." She went over to her car and poured a tall glass of cabernet.

Concerned, Bonnie went over to her. "Missy, is everything all right?"

"Bonnie, I just don't want to be the only girl in this movie who shows her boobs."

"Oh, Missy, you won't be. My daughter Lori already showed hers in a scene months ago."

"Oh. Okay then." She downed the rest of her glass. "Okay, Mike, I'm ready!"

She stepped back into the glare of the headlights and we shot the rest of the scene. I was extremely careful to frame her so that there were no embarrassing or gratuitous displays.

We finished all of Missy's shots by around 8:30, as the night chill was setting in. As Missy was pulling on a sweatshirt David Harris, the professor of a college drama department, told her, "I gotta tell you, you've got more guts than most of my students." Missy was so floored by his compliment I think she could have stayed and danced for us all night no matter how much the temperature dropped.

The next day I pulled a few JPEGs from the night's footage and e-mailed them to Jimmy and Missy to give them an idea of how the shoot turned out. Jimmy immediately wrote me back, "Wow! Who is that? Missy is hot!"

Missy's favorite image from the shoot. Note the $20 bills in the foreground that serve as censor bars.

Lori Foxworth reviews her pole-dancing scene in *Nightbeats*. I was concerned about brief flashes of nudity in some of the shots but Lori responded, "No, no, I like it. I've worked out really hard to get that body. I want *something* to show for it." Circled around the iMac with her are sister Jenna Lincoln and her mother and casting agent Bonnie Bennett.

Scenes involving nudity always have the potential to be embarrassing for women if shot or edited in an exploitive way. To make my actors comfortable I promise that they will get to see their scene first and they get to approve their scene before I use it. So far, I haven't had any complaints.

Working With Non-Actors

I'VE READ MANY INTERVIEWS WITH DIRECTORS who say they like working with non-actors. Danny Boyle did this to spectacular success with *Slumdog Millionaire*. Though it should be noted, once he'd cast his novice actors he put them through months of working with acting coaches to get their performances to the level where he wanted them when they went in front of the cameras.

I strongly believe that the quality of a film is dependent on the quality of its actors. Good actors can make weak writing sing. Reason enough to always strive to work with theatrically trained actors. I confess to having gone against that rule when we cast Missy Bell in *Nightbeats*.

Before working with Missy I'd always found that mixing a "regular person" with an experienced actor resulted in a disjointed scene. Like having a conversation with someone in your living room, then the door bell rings and you answer it to find a salesman trying to hawk carpet cleaner. The flow of the moment is thrown off and it's hard to get back into it again. I feel that way when I watch a movie with a great actor interacting with someone off the street who's just been given some lines to read. The levels are all wrong and it just doesn't work.

But rules are made to be broken. Every once in a while you're talking with someone and something in your gut just kicks in and tells you, "There's something interesting about this person. I think they could pull it off." Call it instinct or chemistry or magic or faith.

In Missy's case there was something about her fearless outgoing personality that inspired Bonnie and myself to believe that she could do it. Also, the role that we asked Missy to play didn't involve any major dramatic scenes with complex dialogue or ranges of emotion. As long as she was relaxed and natural and didn't try to "act" and be somebody else we thought she could be good. (Not to mention her enthusiasm: "I get to be in a movie and have Kitten Natividad kick my ass!")

Intermingling non-actors into scenes with experienced principle cast members only works if the "regular people" simply play "regular people" and are not being expected to play intricate characters.

Finding A Name Actor

"More Stars Than There Are In Heaven."
- MGM Motto

YOU CAST THE BEST ACTORS YOU CAN GET to sell your story to an audience. A cold, hard truth is that, with very rare exception, DVD distribution companies will only pick up films that have at least one recognized name actor whose picture can be featured prominently on the DVD box. For that reason you should anticipate marketing your first film yourself through DVD self-distribution and Internet downloads.

At this point you're probably thinking, "Now he tells me!"

Until you make a film you're just another wannabe, full of talk. Once you *have* made a film, and made a good one, you have the opportunity to reach out to name actors and production companies because you'll have a DVD of a full-length film as an example of what you can do.

There are a number of big-name actors who like to balance high-profile mainstream movies with small independent films. They'll make a blockbuster for Hollywood for a multimillion dollar fee then make an independent film for the sake of art for only the S.A.G. (Screen Actors Guild) minimum of a few hundred dollars a day. Some name actors like helping out small films and emerging filmmakers they believe in, especially if the film can be shot quickly and is about subject matter they are passionate about. If it's a role that might generate festival or Oscar buzz, all the better.

You may have better luck appealing to actors who've made careers playing supporting roles. Entice them with the lead role in a good script that can be shot in just a few weeks and offer an associate producer or co-producer credit. If you can connect with an actor looking for the next step up the ladder you might find a business partner.

An agent once told me how he'd been reading scripts for years, looking for great stories with original plots and characters that he could sell to the studios, until one day he suddenly realized: movies are all about movie stars. He started reexamining the scripts he liked based on whether they had parts for two stars: a man and a woman as romantic leads or two men for a buddy picture or a story with two great antagonists. If he could attach stars to these scripts they'd sell and get made.

In Hollywood it's all about stars. Stars sell movies.

SOUND:
Good Sound Doesn't Happen Twice

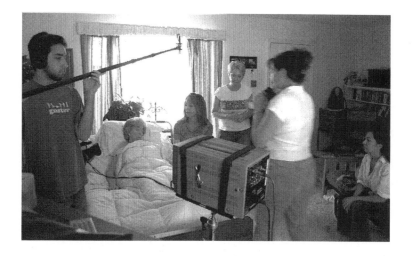

Soundman Dominick Bernal watches the monitor to make sure he has the Oktava mic out of the picture during the deathwatch sequence in *Year.*

Getting The Audio Right—The First Time

> Nothing can kill a movie quicker than bad audio. You shouldn't have to strain to hear what's being said.

YOU CAN ALWAYS TELL THE WORTH OF A FILMMAKER BY HOW THEIR MOVIE SOUNDS. I think of the old low budget drive-in movies recorded with one microphone at the top of a room (to avoid lighting shadows) with dialogue echoing off hard wood walls, making the actors sound like they're in a port-a-potty.

No-Budget Filmmakers' Biggest Audio Mistakes:
- Relying on one boom mic for the primary sound
- Having the least experienced person on the set working the boom
- The boom operator doesn't wear headphones to hear the sound that is being recorded

As a TV news cameraman I'm used to recording multiple channels of sound and having it crystal clean. Since I'm already writing, directing and shooting the film, I know in advance that I'll be the one editing it, and I also know how I want the audio to sound, I might as well go ahead and record that myself too.

Two Actors - Two Wireless Mics - Two XLR Inputs

Almost all of the dialogue in *Year* was recorded with wireless mics, as inspired by Michael Winterbottom's *Wonderland* (U.K., 1999), which had all the actors wearing wireless mics. If you listen closely to *Wonderland* you'll notice that much of the natural sound is also taken from the mics the actors were wearing. In one scene the camera is shooting down a hallway on a woman rummaging through some clothes in a far room and all the sound is coming from her mic.

British filmmaker Terence Davies reviews sequences of *Nightbeats* in the editing studio. Advice to all filmmakers: When a great director says you should cut your scenes down, you do what he tells you.

Terence Davies - Minimalism And Sound

One of our dearest friends is the British film director Terence Davies, whose film *Distant Voices, Still Lives* is considered one of the great British films of the 20th Century. It's a film of haunting images and extraordinary sound. Stark and minimal. I don't think there are ever more than two audio tracks running in the whole film.

One scene that stands out is a single camera setup in medium-long shot of a family on the front stoop of a house, which was an exterior location built in a studio sound stage. There's a little bit of dialogue, some footsteps, the sound of a wallet being removed from a purse and some coins taken out and pressed into a hand. Nothing earth shattering, just a simple one-shot scene, but the sound was pristine.

I mentioned this to Terence, "It sounded like you didn't add anything to the soundtrack. Like it was all just the sound recorded at the moment."

"Oh yes, my dear," Terence confirmed. "I couldn't afford to add anything. We simply didn't have the money. And there was only the one microphone. That's all we ever had. Everything you hear is what we recorded on the set when the camera was rolling."

Record Sound To The Camcorder Or An Audio Recorder?

There have been ongoing arguments whether sound quality is better if it's recorded double-system sound, meaning the old-fashioned method using a clapper board and recording sound into a separate digital recorder and synching up later on the computer, or simply recording the sound straight into the camera and not bothering with post-synching.

Comparison tests conducted with the Sony VX1000, the first prosumer mini-dv camcorder, were done a few years ago where audio was simultaneously recorded directly into the camera as well as separately by a soundman using a DAT recorder. The two recordings were reviewed on waveform monitors and it turned out that there was zero loss in audio quality by recording directly to the camera. This proved that recording sound into a separate digital recorder and synching it up with the picture in post is a lot of extra trouble and completely unnecessary.

Different Mics for Different Scenes

DON'T BELIEVE MOVIE PHOTOS OF HOW SOUND IS RECORDED. When I ask people on inexperienced crews why they're using just one overhead boom mic to record audio I'm usually given a lot of know-it-all attitude, "Because that's how they do it in movies."

After a follow-up question or two I'll find out that their sound recording knowledge is based on behind-the-scenes photos and making-of documentaries of Hollywood crews depicting a soundman wielding a boom pole with a shotgun mic over the scene being filmed.

The truth is that those mics are usually only picking up background sound and not the primary dialogue. On almost every major Hollywood film every actor is wearing a hidden wireless mic to provide clean, crisp audio no matter where they are on the set.

Of course, you never see the wireless mics in the behind-the-scenes footage because they're hidden.

In my equipment bag I have:

> 2 Sony ECM-55 lavalier mics
> 2 Sennheiser EV 100 wireless mics
> 1 Sennheiser MKH 816 shotgun mic

These are all I need to record audio for a film.

Sony ECM 55 Lavelier Microphone

This is a hardline mic that runs on a AA battery. I've used one of these mics for 25 years and it can be your best friend when you're in the trenches.

A lavelier (or "lav") will record more isolated sound than a shotgun. These things are almost indestructible. Like Russian tanks they endure the Battle of Berlin to make a perfect *borscht* on Sunday. (I'm not sure what that means, but you get the picture.)

Sennheiser MKH 816 Shotgun Mic

In 25 years as a TV news cameraman I have shot with lots of different cameras but have always had Sennheiser shotgun mics for recording natural sound.

The ME-80 and 416 are rock solid mics. Get the camera and the mic in a reasonable proximity to your subject and the Sennheiser takes care of you.

I use the Sennheiser 816 for films. Almost twice as long as the 416 at twenty inches, the 816 picks up a much narrower range of sound. If the 816 is pointed directly toward someone talking it will pick them up perfectly, yet someone off to the side will barely be heard.

A friend had loaned me an 816[7] when I was recording sound effects for *Year*. I had the 816 was on a boom pole extended up into a tree during a breezy afternoon to get sound of leaves rustling. (This was when I met Jimmy Bell walking his dog.) The sound of the leaves was the cleanest I'd ever heard. Then I noticed a plane crossing the sky, though I couldn't hear it at all in the headphones. I took the boom out of the tree and angled the 816 up towards the plane. Now I could hear the plane perfectly but the rustling leaves were gone. I bought my own 816 not long after that.

Sennheiser EVolution 100 Wireless Mic System

For almost twenty years I've been using an analog wireless system that originally sold for $3,500. Recently I switched to the Sennheiser EVolution 100 wireless mic system. It's digital, works above and beyond anything I've used before, and is only $500.

Before buying it I did a test with soundman Jimmy Bell, who has several of these. I listened through the wireless receiver hooked up to my JVC GY HD110U inside his recording studio while Jimmy, wearing the transmitter, went outside, through his house and out into the middle of the street out front. Every step of the way he came in perfectly clear, like he was right next to me.

---

[7] Filmmakers are always in need of some piece of equipment and will usually go out of their way to help another filmmaker. Especially someone they trust and whose films they respect.

Wireless mics come in two components:

The Transmitter—A small, palm-
sized box that an actor wears either
on a belt, in a pocket, or taped to
the inside of a leg as many women
do when wearing skirts that don't
have belts or pockets. From this
runs a thin cable leading to a
lavelier mic that's hidden under the
actor's clothes.

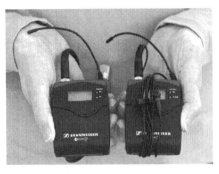

The Receiver—A similar-sized box with antenna(s) for picking up the wireless
signal.

You can also get an audio cable for the transmitter with an XLR input for
connecting to a shotgun mic. Very handy when using a shotgun on a boom
and not wanting miles of cables strewn around.

Most receivers attach to the camcorder's hot shoe to be close to the
XLR inputs on the side of the camera. When I'm using two wireless
systems I may have the second one velcroed to the camera's shoulder
mount or tucked into a vest pocket on a three-foot audio cable.

Each type of mic records sound differently. If you start recording a
scene with one type of mic, whether lavs or overhead shotgun on a
boom, stick with it through the end of the scene for consistency. Don't
mix a lav with a shotgun in the middle of a scene. The difference will
perk up the ears of an audience, and not in a good way.

The Importance Of XLR Audio Inputs

As a general rule I don't trust boom
mics for recording dialogue. I design
the scenes when I'm writing to
primarily be between two people so
that each actor is wearing a wireless or
hardlined mic feeding separately into
the two XLR audio inputs on the
camera[8]. In other words:

    Actor One—Audio Channel One
    Actor Two—Audio Channel Two

---

8 Most higher-end prosumer cameras have two XLR audio inputs.

Smaller Camcorders—Make Sure There's A Stereo Mic Input

Having a stereo mic input will allow you to get an XLR adapter, such as a BeachTek, that can be plugged into your camera through a micro-jack for using professional microphones.

Recording your mics on separate audio channels is crucial. It allows you to separate one actor's audio track from another actor's track, which makes a tremendous difference later in the editing.

I used a BeachTek XLR adaptor on the Sony TRV900 and the sound was fabulous. BeachTek also makes XLR adaptors that hold batteries for providing phantom power, which many of the higher-end mics require.

Overhead Boom Mic—Get It In Close

Lav mics, whether wireless or hardlined to the camera on audio cables, on each actor will record the cleanest dialogue. If a shotgun absolutely must be used get it in as close to the actors as you can. If you have dialogue scenes designed to be filmed in long and medium shots, toss them out and go with medium shots and close-ups instead. Do whatever you have to do to get the cleanest sound you can. Your vision may be compromised, but the audience will be able to hear it better.

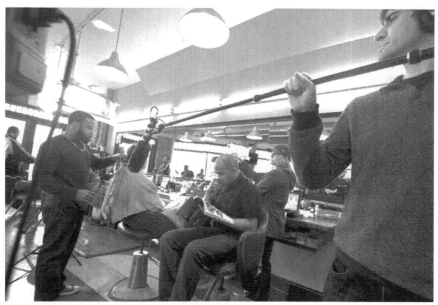

A sound boom operator gets the shotgun mic in close for a take on the set of *Stolen Moments*, directed by Elisabeth Nunziato. In the center is actor Anthony D'Juan, who was one of the leads in *Nightbeats*.

Always Wear Good Headphones

Don't skimp on cheap headphones with thin small foam pads. I use Sennheiser HD 280 headphones that I pick up at music stores for around $100. They're sturdy and fit snugly around my ears, isolating the sound so well that when someone tries to talk to me I have to take them off to hear.

> NOTE: When buying high-end headphones, music stores may try to sell you a replacement insurance policy. What they don't tell you, and usually don't know, is that the insurance only covers the headphones and not the jack, which is the most likely component to break. So save the twenty or thirty bucks for the policy and use it toward your next set of headphones.

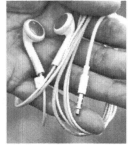

> For documentary work where you're trying to be surreptitious use earbuds that won't attract attention.

> Know the sound you're getting when you're shooting it because you can never get it back.

Hard Walls & Echoes

With interior settings the sound quality varies from room to room depending on hard walls, hard wood or cement floors and low ceilings. Audio will bounce all over those hard surfaces making it difficult, if not impossible to record dialogue cleanly.

SOLUTION: Put up two C-stands and drape a blanket between them. Shoot the actors in close shots with the blanket close off to the side. This will help sponge up some of the echoing and make the sound a little clearer.

Lavelier Mics For One To Two Actors

There's a scene in John Cassavetes' *A Woman Under The Influence* with Peter Falk riding in the back of a moving truck and drinking beer with his kids. The sound is perfect and not one word was looped. It was achieved by using lavelier mics hidden under the actors' clothes with hardline cables running out their pants legs to the recorder.

The beauty of a lavelier mic, whether it's wireless or cabled, is that it's within inches of an actor's mouth.

The closer the mic, the cleaner the audio.

Boom Mics For Groups

For *Year* we only had one morning and afternoon to shoot the whole opening six-minute New Year's Eve party sequence. With over a dozen separate speaking parts and several scenes with four and five people talking at a time, rotating the two wireless mics from actor to actor was not going to be practical. So instead of two wireless lavs we used two Sennheiser shotgun mics on boom poles.

To run the handheld boom I enlisted Dominick Bernal, a young filmmaker and musician. Dominick would have his boom directed towards the actors speaking on one side of the camera while the actors on the other side were covered with a static shotgun mic extended on a boom pole that was fixed to a C-stand. Both shotgun mics fed into the XLR jacks on the side of the Panasonic DVX100A. Dominick would follow my shot on the monitor to see how close he could get his mic to the actors to get the cleanest sound.

During these scenes the extras were directed to look like they were talking but to not make a sound. Later we did several takes of people talking and mingling as if they were at a real party, which was layered under the dialogue scenes as background. Not one word of any of the actors' dialogue had to be dubbed in. In fact, only a handful of lines in the entire film were re-recorded.

Cutting To The Chase: Separate Audio Channels & Editing

When editing dialogue scenes, the sound is much clearer by only having the sound up from the actor who is talking. When that actor finishes their line I bring their audio down completely and bring up the audio of the other actor for their line.

This is done for every single line of dialogue in the movie. It sounds laborious but it pays off. At the San Francisco Independent Film Festival several filmmakers who'd spent as much as $30,000 for their post sound mixes asked where I'd taken *Year* to be mixed because the sound and dialogue was so clean.

"I just used separate wireless mics plugged straight into the camera and adjusted all the levels on the Final Cut Pro timeline."

"That's it? You didn't take it to a post house?"

They'd been taught in film school that they had to have a soundman, double-system sound and an audio mix at a post-production house. All that stuff can be really nice but if it's not recorded properly in the first place nothing is going to matter.

The four Stone sisters having Sunday afternoon visit on the patio in *Year*. A sound recording situation where an overhead boom mic would have picked up every distracting ambient sound in the neighborhood. To solve that problem each actor was wearing their own lavelier mic.

Multiple Mics & "Y" Cables

There's a scene in *Year* involving the four Stone sisters drinking wine and talking on a backyard patio. Trying to record this exterior setting with a shotgun mic on a boom would have picked up far too much background audio from surrounding yards, street traffic, wind, etc. Instead, I used my two Sony ECM-55 lavelier mics and two others that I borrowed from a filmmaker friend.

On one side of the patio were Gina (Katherine Pappa) and Vivian (Carol Miranda) and sitting across from them were Ava (Bonnie Bennett) and Sidney (Christine Nicholson). Each had a Sony ECM-55 lav mic run up inside their blouses, clipped to the space in the middle of their bras.

Carol's and Katherine's lavelier mics were at the end of a pair of twenty foot long audio cables that fed into a "Y" cable, and Bonnie's and Christine's lavelier mics fed over another set of cables into another "Y" cable.

They're called "Y" cables because they look like a "Y." It allows you to plug two mics into the "Y" end combining the sound into a single channel of audio. This permitted me to have four separate Sony ECM-55 lav mics mixed together through two "Y" cables, which were then plugged into the Panasonic DVX100A's two side XLR inputs.

Filming In A Stationary Car

There's a scene in *Nightbeats* with Bonnie Bennett and Lori Foxworth, playing a lounge singer and a junkie stripper, shot inside a parked car with the windows rolled up to baffle the sound outside. Each was wearing a Sony ECM-55 lav mic hardlined to cables feeding out through the closed driver's door to the XLR inputs on the side of the JVC GY HD110U camcorder. I was outside the car shooting in through the windows.

It was a Friday night and not far away down the alley was a bar with music spilling out, yet through the headphones everything sounded fine. Throughout the evening people would be coming out of the bar, going to their cars and driving off and every time I'd be biting my lip thinking, "Crap, that's gonna mess up this take."

After we got home and I'd loaded the footage into Final Cut and started reviewing the takes I was amazed to find that the sound was perfect. As it turned out, having the car windows rolled up had completely eliminated the outside street sounds.

Wireless Lav Mic For Picking Up Detail Sounds

In any contemporary film these days there's a scene with someone typing at a computer. One thing I always do is place a wireless mic off to the side of the keyboard to pick up the *click-click-click* of the keys being typed. When shooting a long shot of an actor in the middle of an office or on a park bench, this clear typing sound will make the character stand out and help the audience know where to look.

Don't Forget The "Room Tone"—Both Interior & Exterior

Room tone is recorded at an interior or exterior location after the shooting's finished and the crew's moved on. The soundman stays behind and records a few minutes of ambient sound of the location. It might be the sound of traffic from a street outside, of a ventilation system or air conditioner, a backyard with birds chirping, leaves rustling in a breeze, or just the hiss of an empty room.

You can be sitting in a room and swear there's not a sound to be had, but pull out a good microphone, record for a couple minutes and play it back and there actually *is* something going on there.

There are two scenes in *Year* that take place at an outdoor cafe. In the first scene, Brendan (Blair Leatherwood), who is married to Ava (Bonnie Bennett), the eldest of the Stone sisters, is having coffee with his current lover (Cheantell Munn), when he's spotted by Ava's sister

Sidney (Christine Nicholson). In a follow-up scene Sidney returns to the cafe and again finds Brendan, whom she's never cared for, having coffee by himself and reading the paper at one of the outside bistro tables. She joins him and they have a contemptuous conversation, which sparks the groundwork for an affair between them.

These two scenes were shot on successive Sunday mornings at an actual cafe run by college students near our house. As long as we weren't disruptive to their clientele everything was cool. By shooting without a tripod and without a crew, with just the actors on wireless microphones and me with the handheld Panasonic DVX 100A, we were virtually under the radar. The customers were incredibly cooperative without having to be asked, sitting away from us so their conversations rarely ever bled over into our sound. The only sound beyond our control was traffic from the boulevard and some birds.

Over the next few weeks I edited the footage in Final Cut Pro, but due to the inconsistent flows of traffic in the background under the actors' dialogue, the sound of the scenes was coming out patchy and uneven.

As an experiment I returned to the cafe, set the Panasonic camcorder on the roof of my car with a Sennheiser 416 shotgun mic and recorded fifteen minutes of traffic sound. I loaded the new audio into the computer, played it under the scenes and now the background traffic sound was even and the scenes played fine. I breathed a huge sigh of relief and uncorked a very nice bottle of wine.

Room tone can save a scene when cutting it together later.

Putting Mics On Actors

IF THE ACTORS ARE GOING TO BE MOVING AROUND, as opposed to sit down dialogue where cabled mics are fine, put a wireless mic on each actor. It allows them to be free and within minutes they'll forget about the mic and the transmitter they're wearing and just focus on their performance.

> I keep a couple thin strips of gaffer's tape on the side of the camera so I can quickly grab one when mic'ing actors.

Mic'ing Male Actors

Men are easy. Their clothes are mostly made out of cotton and usually you'll be dealing with either a button-up shirt with a collar or a T-shirt. Put a strip of gaffer's tape around the top of the mic and tape it to the inside of the shirt nearest their mouth, being careful not to bunch up the shirt with the tape and make the mic visible.

Filming With Open-Collared Shirts

If the mic is taped inside a shirt or blouse that has the top few buttons undone pay close attention when filming to make sure the mic can't be seen. When you change camera angles it may be necessary to move the mic to the other side.

Mic'ing Female Actors

In a no-budget film your actors wear their own clothes. Stress to them to wear blouses, tops and dresses made out of cotton. *No silk or polyester.* These fabrics make scratchy sounds when they rub together. Cotton is softer and virtually silent.

Women will want to look their best on camera, meaning formfitting clothes that will not easily permit a mic to be hidden beneath the fabric.

On women the most practical location to place a mic is at the apex of their bra between the cups. The shape of the breasts holds the fabric of their clothing out from the mic allowing for perfect sound recording.

If your actor wears a sports bra that is flat across the front make the actor aware that she will have to run the mic up the inside of her sports bra and clip it in the gap between her breasts.

Be tactful, straightforward and professional with female actors. Explain everything in advance so they can plan their wardrobe, both outer and under garments that they can be comfortable in.

On the first day of filming with a new female actor I'll say, "I'll need you to run this mic up underneath your shirt and then use this piece of gaffer's tape to tape the mic to the middle of your bra." The actor will turn her back or go into another room for a moment, then come back and I'll do an audio check to make sure everything is right and we'll shoot the scene.

Quite often, after a day of this when they're comfortable with me, the actor will simply open her shirt enough and let me position the mic where it will work best on her bra.

Depending on the style of the bra and how close the cups are to where the mic needs to be taped I will only hold the mic to the place where it needs to be and have the woman press the tape down to secure it.

Don't Talk Technical With Your Actors

Unless specifically asked I never talk about my equipment, how expensive it is or how it works. Keep all your focus on the actors and the scene at hand.

Decorum & Working In Delicate Situations

Both *Year* and *Nightbeats* are strong stories about women involving delicate dramatic situations so it was essential that the actors' on-set experience was comfortable and that conduct was totally appropriate at all times. I also like to have another woman present for reassurance.

It's absolutely vital to maintain a high level of propriety. An actor might make a little *double entendre* to break the tension, such as, "You must really enjoy this part." It's one thing for an actor to say something like this as a stress reliever but it is imperative that you should not participate. Stay totally professional. Smile politely and ask for a mic check. Actors will judge you by how you handle moments like this and respect you for keeping focused on the work.

On *Power*, the short film I shot for Michael Dryhurst, there was a scene of people playing strip poker. We had just two lavelier mics that we moved from actor to actor as we filmed their individual two-shots and close-ups. One actress's costume was a black lace bra and panties that required running the mic cable up inside the lace of one of her bra cups. Fortunately, my wife Bonnie was also one of the actors in the scene and this provided a comfort level for the woman.

EDITING: Where The Film Is Made

On The Chopping Block

> The first part of editing is easy: Cut out everything that's crap.

IN SCREENWRITING A STORY IS ADAPTED INTO A SCREENPLAY. In editing the footage is adapted into a film. Just as a story goes through many changes to become a workable script editing works the same way, only instead of working with words you're working with shots, takes and sound. Lines will be dropped, scenes deleted or moved around any number of ways until the film is finished. This is why experienced writer-directors say editing is the final draft of the screenplay.

Once I start cutting I never look back at the script. Whatever was written on the page is no longer important. All that matters is making something out of the footage that's there.

The Most Brilliantly Edited Films I've Ever Seen:

The Black Stallion	Carroll Ballard
Never Cry Wolf	Carroll Ballard
Apocalypse Now	Francis Ford Coppola, Walter Murch
The French Connection	William Friedkin
Lawrence of Arabia	David Lean
The Landlord	Hal Ashby
The Thomas Crown Affair	Hal Ashby
Coming Home	Hal Ashby

I Don't Do Dailies, I Just Start Cutting

The minute I get home from a shoot I go straight to the Mac and load everything into Final Cut, then back it up onto a second external hard drive. I load everything. Even a poor take may have a good line reading, facial look, reaction, or little bit of business that can make a scene spark.

I drag all the new footage onto the timeline and review the takes, going by gut reactions, and right from the very first take I start cutting, keeping the good stuff and deleting everything else.

I don't cut in any textbook style, such as:

ESTABLISHING SHOT: Show where we are.
MEDIUM SHOT: Character walks up.
P.O.V.: What character sees.

This is old-hat and deathly predictable. Audiences are far too cinema-literate and need to be continually surprised and stimulated. I'll cut from anything to anything as long as it works. There are no hard-and-fast rules. You just have to do the work. The more you edit the more perceptive your instincts become.

When I cut scenes with actors everything is based on performance. As I review takes, when I see something that could look good with something in an earlier take I'll make the edit right then and there. I don't want to run the risk of forgetting about it.

By the time I've finished reviewing all the takes I will have already made many preliminary edits. Then I begin putting the good elements that I have left together, crosscutting and trimming, editing for performance, emotion and rhythm.

I used to think that movies were all about writing and cinematography. Now I see them as being all about editing and performance. If your actors don't have the magic, then no technical wizardry will save the film.

Protect Yourself—Back-Up Everything

In 25 years of shooting news I've covered enough house fires and break-ins to have learned that you don't keep all your hard drives under the same roof.

- Hard drives can fail at any time.
- Always, always, always back-up footage and audio clips.
- Back-up all your material to a second drive.
- For shooting tapeless, back-up to a third hard drive.
- Don't store the back-up drives under the same roof as the master drive.
- If you're editing in a rented office space, take a drive home with you. Break-ins happen all the time and electronics are the primary items to be stolen.
- If editing at home, put the back-up drive out in the garage, in your car, or take it to work and store it in a desk drawer or locker. But keep it in a completely different location.
- Protect your footage like the gold at Fort Knox.
- Without the footage the film is dead.

Organize, Organize, Organize

The single most important element about post-production is keeping all the sound and video files *organized*. You have to have the attention to detail of a certified public accountant and the organizational skills of a librarian. I use the scene numbers in the shooting script to organize my footage, then individually number each shot and piece of separate sound within that scene number. It's then easy to find the footage numerically.

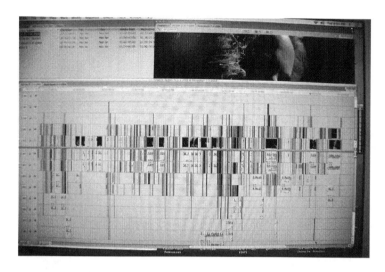

The final thirty minutes of *Nightbeats* on the Final Cut Pro timeline. The vertical rectangles above the center horizontal dividing line are shots and below are the corresponding audio files. Many beginning filmmakers are afraid of the editing process, but once you get started that's where you want to spend all your time.

Nonlinear Editing

In digital editing it's all about the timeline. Your footage goes onto the "timeline" where there's a track for video and two tracks for audio: for Channel One Audio and Channel Two Audio. Additional tracks of video and audio can be added so shots can be layered on top of each other and moved around, creating the scenes.

Magical Mistakes

I'm always hoping for those special moments in a shoot when an actor gets so involved that they take a scene to a different place.

In *Nightbeats* there's a long dialogue scene between Lori Foxworth and Kelly Nixon where Lori got so emotionally involved during one take that she forgot a couple of her lines but kept on going. When I edited the scene I crosscut between several different takes to work those lines back in.

Later when the film was all assembled I was looking for unnecessary and redundant lines to cut out, trimming the fat. I came to the Lori-Kelly scene and started dropping a few shots here, a line there, and looked at that take of Lori's again.

The intensity on Lori's face when she dropped the lines was so compelling that I wound up reworking the scene once more so that, instead of cutting to other shots, I just held on that close-up of Lori for twenty-five seconds. Suddenly the scene transcended from being good to having magic, a rare quality that can't be created in the editing but can only come from the talent of the actors and being an observant editor to recognize it.

A Film's Style Comes In The Editing

Necessity dictates that I shoot scenes out of chronological order, therefore I also edit scenes out of order. By cutting scenes right after shooting them I can see what shots are working better than others, two shots or close-ups or medium close-ups, and I start shooting more of these as filming progresses.

Be Ruthless With Your Footage

Being your own editor demands removing yourself from every other aspect of the film and focusing entirely on shaping a movie out of the footage you have.

My friend and collaborator Michael Dryhurst told me many times about working on films where days were spent shooting sequences costing hundreds of thousands of dollars only to discover in the editing room that the sequence wasn't necessary.

Don't be afraid *not* to use material.

The same rules for writing also apply to editing: the more you cut, the better what remains looks.

If I cut a scene to the bone, then later begin to reassess, "God, I should've kept that shot in," it's still in the computer, I can always put it back. Those cherished scenes that you deleted can always go into the DVD extras—Ridley Scott does.

Be completely honest with yourself. Self-delusion is fatal to an artist. Ask yourself:

> Am I holding on this shot too long?
> Would the scene benefit from cutting to another actor's reaction?
> Have I fallen in love with my own work?

Cut On Action & Distract With Sound

Watch some of Frank Capra's films with the sound off. Nothing matches. From one shot to the next is an endless array of jump cuts. However, turn the volume back up and you see that by cutting on sound it all flows.

For example:

> SHOT: A PERSON at a table wrapping a present.
> CLOSER SHOT: THE PERSON'S HANDS folding wrapping paper.

You can make a smooth cut between these two shots, even if the action of the hands from the first shot to the second shot doesn't match the action, by cutting on the strong crinkling sound of the paper being folded.

Similarly, when cutting a dialogue scene where the physical action is not matching, make the cuts at the beginning of the next person's lines. If the next shot also doesn't match make another hard cut at the beginning of the next line of dialogue. To help smooth out the sound even more layer some background audio over the scene, such as traffic sounds from outside, an airplane or helicopter passing overhead.

Using an audio fade between shots, which can be found in the effects menu, can also help to smooth out the sound. An audio fade works as a dissolve between two bits of audio. Once you hear how much nicer your cuts work with audio fades between them, you'll want to use them every time.

Using your sound effectively will help tremendously to make your images transition from one to the other more smoothly. Just watch a few well-edited movies with the sound off and you'll be amazed how much the action differs from one shot to the next.

> TO MAKE UNMATCHING SHOTS CUT SEAMLESSLY:

Attract the attention of the viewer's ears &
Distract the attention of the viewer's eyes.

If The Shot Isn't Close Enough—Blow It Up

When I was in the final stages of editing of *Nightbeats* there were
several scenes that I wished I'd framed tighter when I'd shot them.
Then on the timeline I started experimenting by blowing the shots up
10%, 20%, 30%, even 50% to get tighter on the faces, taking a loose
medium-close shot and magnifying it into a close shot to more
emotionally involve the audience.

In one sequence where I wanted a very rapid series of super-fast and
disorienting cuts I even went so far as to blow up some shots 100% and
150%. A few shots did look a little grainy, but they were very fleeting
and reminded me of the grittiness of *The French Connection*, which
was fine with me.

Edit, Edit, Edit

Just because you've cut your scene once doesn't mean it's finished.
When a scene is stitched together with other scenes into ten and fifteen
minute sequences you start to see what's working and what needs to be
cut down even more or cut out completely.

Editing gives you the chance to fix the mistakes you're now aware you
made in the writing and shooting stages. Scenes that worked fine on
paper can now look quite different when you see them played out. You
might come to find that the order of the actors' lines could have been
better. That you missed a shot or two when you were shooting because
your focus was on some other aspect of the scene. That you didn't
realize the business the actor was doing with their hands is now
distracting and doesn't quite fit. In this final stage of putting together
the footage into creating a movie you have to challenge yourself to
rethink what you were thinking before and be open to new possibilities
to make it work.

Just because it's written one way or shot one way doesn't
mean it has to stay that way.

Keep Short Films Short: 10 Minutes Or Less

The shorter the better. Film festivals want to pack in as many films as
they can. If your short film is fifteen minutes long and it's on equal par
with two eight minute films a festival programmer may go with the
other two so they can squeeze more titles into the program roster.

Feature Films: 90 Minutes Or Less—75 Is Better

A misconception among many first-time filmmakers is that a feature has to be 90 minutes long. If their film comes in at 75 or 80 minutes they'll shoot additional scenes and extend others to stretch it out to an hour and a half. End result: their film is not nearly as good.

A feature can be anything over 70 minutes. Some festivals even classify 65 minutes as the feature minimum. *Tadpole*, directed by Gary Winick and starring Sigourney Weaver, shot on Sony PD 150 camcorders, ran only 73 minutes, nine of which were closing credits. It went on to win the Audience Favorite and Best Director prizes at the 2005 Sundance Film Festival and sold for $4.5 million.

Steven Soderbergh (*Sex, Lies & Videotape, Traffic, Ocean's 11*) has made two films, *Bubble* and *The Girlfriend Experience*, which are both only 75 minutes.

When I bring this up to friends who've tried their hands at a feature they'll often point out, "But, Mike, *Year* was over 100 minutes long."

"True, but that's only *after* I cut it down from 150 minutes."

A 90-minute or less feature allows festival programmers to stack a short or two in with your film and makes for a quicker turnaround time for the next movie.

I talked with a woman who programmed a Los Angeles festival who once lamented, "Why is it you filmmakers are always making movies that are over 100 minutes long? Keep it down to 80 minutes so I can put more films in!"

With that in mind, I kept *Nightbeats* to only 89 minutes.

British filmmaker Shane Meadows established himself as a leading voice in U.K. cinema with *Once Upon A Time In The Midlands* and *This Is England*, which won the B.A.F.T.A. for Best British Film. His more recent films have been simpler stories that Meadows has said were only as long as they needed to be: *Somers Town* and *Le Donk & Scor-zay-zee* were both only 71 minutes.

I'd like to try keeping the next film to 75 minutes with credits. Maybe then I could make it in one year instead of the two years it's typically taken.

Animated "Production Company" Logos & Opening Credits

It never ceases to amaze me to be at a festival and see so many films start out with elaborate computer-animated graphics showing off the name of their production company, then following it with a film that's a bunch of crap.

Do your film a favor and keep the titles and credits simple and put your time and effort into making a good film.

Woody Allen has used the same credits, even the same font, for over thirty years: a simple black screen with credits in white cutting on and off. He doesn't even use fades or dissolves, just straight cuts. Simple, cheap, does the job.

Start your movie with a company credit and title in simple lettering, then give the audience a movie that's worth their time.

Opening Actor Credits—Who Are These People?

Another thing that drives me crazy at festivals is watching movies that open with somber piano music followed by cast credits in big letters of people nobody's ever heard of. How am I going to know who is who when none of these people have ever been in a movie before? It's one thing if the credits say Gene Hackman or Nicole Kidman, but when they're a couple people who work part-time at a Seven Eleven in Boise who the hell cares?

Save the credits for the end of the movie and credit the actors' names alongside a clip from the film so the audience can see who they are and then they'll have a reason to applaud.

Credits—Keep 'em Lean

Don't spread your name around a dozen times for every job you did, like "casting," "camera operator," "craft services," "accounting," etc. If someone helped me with casting or sound or locations I give them the credit. Nobody's getting paid so at least give them that much.

My name only appears twice in a film:

Producers   Bonnie Bennett   Mike Carroll
Script-director-camera-editor   Mike Carroll

Then a reprise of the film's title, the company name and copyright, all on the same screen, and final fade out. Audiences like brevity.

Jimmy Bell works on the sound design for *Nightbeats* in 3rd Bedroom Studios.

Post-Production Audio—Adding Sound Effects

APPROACH EACH FILM WITH A CONCEPT about how it should be shot and how it should sound.

The sound for *Year* was simple and minimal. There were enough characters and story lines that it didn't need to be complex.

One of the few sounds I did add was ice tinkling. In the scene where Miles (Eric Wheeler) visits Ava (Bonnie Bennett) and they talk over glasses of iced tea, their wireless mics picked up the dialogue perfectly but I felt the sound of their glasses should have been a bit more pronounced.

With the Panasonic DVX-100A and the Sennheiser 416 I recorded sounds of tea pouring into a glass, the thunk of a glass being set down on a counter and the tinkling of ice cubes swirling in a glass. I loaded these into Final Cut Pro and layered different ones at different audio levels under the scene. It then played imperceptibly, as if everything had been recorded during the original shoot. Not light sabers and photon blasters, just subtle sounds added to enrich the scene. But I cannot tell you how many people have commented that the tinkling iced tea glasses made them want something cold to drink.

Looping

I don't like to loop. I don't think it looks believable in digital video, even when it's 24p. Don't take that as a rule, I may just not be good at it.

A couple of lines in *Year* were re-recorded when Vivian (Carol Miranda) goes into her mother's room and finds her passed out. These were played against the back of Carol's head as she approaches her mother's bed so I didn't have to worry about lip-synching. I re-recorded the lines with Carol going through the same motions in a similar-sized room in my house so the sound would match. Aside from that, all the rest of the actors' sound was recorded "live" when we filmed their scenes.

"Live" ADR—Pulling Replacement Sound From Other Takes

A big advantage to using theatre actors is that once they've run through their lines a couple of times their cadence becomes locked in, like a musical performance, and some line deliveries can be virtually identical from take to take.

This saved me a couple of times when I was editing *Year* and heard weird sound flaws ("audio farts" in industry lingo) in the line delivery of an actor's on-camera take. As an experiment I pulled the actor's line from a different take where I was filming a reverse on a different actor and laid that in on the Final Cut timeline over the line that was flawed. To my amazement it matched perfectly. This happened three or four times on *Year* and each time pulling a line from another take did the trick.

> NOTE: These lines were only four or five words long, not a whole paragraph, but for small glitches try the simplest solution first.

Music

The Music Of *Year*

At the beginning of the book I described creating a concept video for *Year* using music that my friend Tom DuHain had discovered on the website of the independent music label Spotted Peccary Music (spottedpeccary.com). I ordered Erik Wøllo's CD *Wind Journey* and used it under my early time-lapse footage of clouds as a presentation video of my concept for the film.

The music of *Wind Journey* was exactly what I was looking for. Internal, atmospheric, almost spiritual at times. It made me think of Michael Nyman's score for Michael Winterbottom's *Wonderland*, one of the truly great motion picture scores.

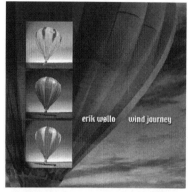

Album cover of *Wind Journey* by Erik Wøllo. Image courtesy of Spotted Peccary Music (spottedpeccary.com).

Hiring a composer or musicians for an original score was totally outside of what I could afford. For a while I was considering classical music because that is in public domain, then hiring students at a music academy to perform it for me. My dilemma was that as much as I know about film, I know virtually nothing about music. My favorite music, quite honestly, is motion picture soundtracks. So I decided not to worry about it for the time being. I was only just starting the movie and there was still another year or so of shooting and editing ahead of me. Plenty of time to worry about that later. In the meantime I'd use Erik Wøllo's *Wind Journey* as a scratch track, temporary music to cut the movie to, then replace at the end.

By late summer 2004 *Year* was moving forward. I had 20 or 30 hours of footage loaded into the computer and had edited enough scenes that I was starting to link them together to build small chunks of the film. This was where I needed music. Too many no-budget movies rely on dialogue to tell the story. I wanted *Year* to be more cinematic, telling the story visually, which demands other sounds for the audience to hear during stretches without dialogue. Finding the right music for that could elevate the film to another level.

There's always been an argument among filmmakers about the role music plays in a film. Some don't like it at all, feeling it comes out of nowhere and distracts from the story. Others rely on it too heavily to add drama and tension to hold the audience's attention.

I lean to the third side of the argument, which regards music as a third character in the movie alongside the actors and the camera, to tell the story. I like the music to convey a mood of what a character is thinking or feeling and let the audience pick it up on an emotional or subconscious level. Sounds kind of lofty but I feel that editing works on the viewer in a psychological way. Dialogue tells the story verbally and editing and music tell the mind what to be focusing on.

This third point of view is extremely effective when using "found music," meaning preexisting music, such as vocals like Frank Sinatra, or rock, or how Stanley Kubrick used classical recordings for *2001: A Space Odyssey.*

I don't think any filmmaker was better at incorporating found music than Hal Ashby and the way he integrated popular music, such as Cat Stevens into *Harold And Maude*, or used late-60s rock in *Coming Home.* In contrast to most filmmakers who use rapid-cutting to follow the beat of the music, Ashby preferred to use music over shots that he would hold on, making the audience have to really look at what is happening in a scene.

Editing to Erik Wollø's music as my scratch track was fantastic. Whatever mood I was looking for there was always a track on *Wind Journey* that fit perfectly. It was almost as if *Wind Journey* had been a soundtrack score. This was when I started to get worried. The movie was working so well with Wollø's music that I found myself falling in love with it. Where would I be able to find music as good to replace it with?

I went back to my friend Tom, who had found the music in the first place, and explained my dilemma. "It's an independent label," Tom said. "Why don't you just call them up, explain what you're doing and ask if you can use it? The worst they could do is say no."

The thought of calling a record company to ask to use their music in my little film sounded crazy. Why should they? But, as Tom pointed out, what did I have to lose? I sent Spotted Peccary Music an e-mail introducing myself as an independent filmmaker and asked to discuss using some of their music in a film I was making. Very quickly a response came from Howard Givens, the president of the company, saying to give him a call.

As it turned out Givens had worked in the film industry and been involved with a couple of independent films himself, so he knew exactly what I was talking about and said he'd be glad to work with me. He said

I just needed to decide which artists I wanted to work with and he would work out the costs for the studio time.

I started to get a little nervous here, having no idea how the music world worked. I explained that I wasn't interested in any new recordings or original music, that I was really only interested in Erik Wollø's *Wind Journey* and using that for the whole soundtrack. To this Gibbons replied, "Oh. Well, if you're only talking about using already existing music then you're welcome to anything in our library."

"You mean . . . it's all right with you if I use *Wind Journey* for the soundtrack of my film?"

"Sure. At this stage I'd say just go ahead. Make your film and keep me posted on its progress. When you get a whole cut with the music laid down send me a copy and we'll go from there. If it gets to a stage where the film gets picked up and is going to be released, then we'll have to work out some sort of compensation. But for the time being go ahead."

It was one of the easiest conversations I'd ever had. Every roadblock in my path had been lifted.

I hung up and looked across to Bonnie. "We got the music."

Bonnie looked back at me, her mouth open, eyes wide. "The whole thing?"

Almost in a daze I replied, "Yeah."

"How much?"

"Nothing."

"Amazing," was all Bonnie could say.

The next day I filled Tom in on the conversation and the outcome, to which he said, "You see, you never know what can happen if you don't ask."

Now that I had the green light to use the music I felt a huge weight had been lifted. Cutting scenes with Erik Wollø's *Wind Journey* was pure joy. I couldn't imagine the picture without it.

By the summer of 2005 I had a completed edit of *Year* and sent it off to Howard Givens so he could see how I'd treated his artist's work. Time passed and I didn't hear anything back. Then in November we got the call informing us that *Year* had been accepted into the 2006 San Francisco Independent Film Festival kicking off in February. I sent an e-mail to Howard with the good word. Two weeks before the premiere came an e-mail response that we needed to talk.

"Oh, shit," was my first reaction. Was he having second thoughts? Did he not like how I'd used the music? There wasn't any time to find anything else. Also, the permission he'd given me had been verbal. I didn't have anything in writing.

So I picked up the phone and held my breath. The first thing Howard said was that he really liked the movie. That he'd watched it a couple times and was amazed how well Erik Wollø's *Wind Journey* worked with the story and that I had thoroughly respected his artist. He was very excited for the screening at the film festival and said for me to be prepared to be approached by distributors for DVD, cable, or whatever, and that if the film started generating money we'd need to work out some sort of arrangement that would be fair. I completely agreed and asked what he thought that should be. Howard said that he did not want to dictate terms, that he respected me as a filmmaker, believed I was honest, and that I should come up with what I thought was fair. I suggested a percentage of any earnings the film might make, which he agreed to and that was it.

Then I asked Howard how it normally worked out when filmmakers approached him about using music, because he was so cooperative from the very beginning without ever having seen anything of what we were doing. His answer really surprised me. He said that he was often approached by filmmakers looking for music for their films and that, just as with me, he tended to grant them permission for the time being. Then he went on to say that of all the filmmakers he'd been approached by I was the only one who'd ever finished their film.

The Music Of *Nightbeats*

Nightbeats was a completely different story. When I met soundman Jimmy Bell, when I was out in the front yard recording the sound of leaves for *Year*, he had just completed a course in ProTools and audio engineering. He and his wife Missy came to the premiere in San Francisco and were big supporters of the film. In addition to wanting to break into doing location sound work for film and TV, which he's since done with great success, he was dying to do the post-production audio and sound design for a film. The sound for *Year* was very natural and minimal, but I knew that with the next film, whatever that wound up being, I wanted to have a much more complex and multilayered soundtrack. "Anything you want to do with the next one," Jimmy jumped in, "count me in. I'd love to do it for you."

When Bonnie and I decided on *Nightbeats* as our next film Jimmy was totally on board. "Strippers, junkies, losers," Jimmy said. "What's not to love?"

To keep the subject matter from being too much of a downer I wrote it to have a lush mixture of music. Some would be songs recorded live with Bonnie and music arranger David Blanchard in a club. The rest needed to be band music, hard electric rock. Jimmy's from the rock world, having toured in a band, so I left it to him to find all of the pre-existing music. This was a Godsend because, again, I know nothing about the music scene.

Jimmy was friends with a few bands based in San Diego and gave me a CD with a couple of tracks he thought night work. I popped them into the player and they were exactly what I was looking for -- hard-driving, blood-pounding electric beats. I loaded them into the Mac and started cutting.

Just as with Tom DuHain finding Erik Wollø's *Wind Journey* for *Year* right out of the gate, Jimmy had found the perfect rock songs for *Nightbeats* on the first try.

He also gave me a CD made by a musician couple who lived in the neighborhood of a soundtrack they'd done for a local indie film that had been rejected. It was electronic, moody and downbeat—exactly the sound I wanted for the scenes where Mercy's strung out on heroin. I loaded it into the Mac immediately. A few days later the couple came by, saw how well their music worked with the Mercy scenes and were on board.

Jimmy also created a number of his own atmospheric sounds, produced with electric guitars, to create a moody aural tapestry.

Once I had the film edited I exported all the sound on the Final Cut Pro timeline out to an external hard drive, which Jimmy loaded into Pro Tools for his final remix and sound design. I have to confess that this was something new for me. On *Year* I did every single aspect of the editing from loading the raw footage

Jimmy Bell smoothes out one of Anthony D'Juan and David Harris's dialogue scenes on the Pro Tools timeline for *Nightbeats.*

into the Mac to exporting the finished film. This time around I was handing the sound over to someone else to work on. And then I had to wait.

When you have thousands of bits of sound on a timeline it takes a while to go through them all, tweak them, equalize, fade, mix in other sounds and adjust everything to the right audio levels. Jimmy, like me, works for a living and was doing this in his spare time. During those months I revamped the film's website and transcribed fourteen hours of audio recordings of a course I taught on independent filmmaking, which became the rough draft for this book.

Then it was into Jimmy's studio, 3rd Bedroom Studios (3rdbedroomstudios.com), for many days of listening to the scenes and adjusting levels. Long, painstaking work. Deadly boring to any outsider looking in, but absolutely vital to getting the sound clean and perfect. I'd never collaborated with anyone that closely before and Jimmy's level of dedication and commitment was total. He was an incredible ally to have working with me towards the same goal.

The Rough Cut—The First Time You See Your Film

A rough cut, or an "assembly," is a stringing together of every scene from beginning to end to see what the film looks like. This is the first time you see the movie, how it's working, and what to fix.

WHEN I FIRST START CUTTING FOOTAGE TOGETHER INTO A SCENE I know it will probably be far too long and that I'll have to lose shots and lines of dialogue by the end. The honest truth about making a movie is that you have no real idea of how it's going to look until you've got it all cut. But you're never going to find that out until you start cutting. The important thing is to not wait around. Jump in and start cutting as soon as you've got footage to load into the computer.

To help create mood I'll pull generic tones and sound effects from Sound Track Pro, which comes with Final Cut Pro, knowing full well that I won't use any of these prepackaged effects in the final version of the film. But it helps to get the show on the road.

Editing Your Film For Time & Rushing To Judgment

The version of *Year* that is available on DVD is seven minutes longer than the version that played in the San Francisco Independent Film Festival.

The first full assembly of *Year* in February 2005 ran 153 minutes. This was after already dropping over twenty minutes of scenes because they didn't work. To get a check of what was working and what wasn't I ran this rough cut for Bonnie Bennett and Michael Dryhurst.

When you watch a rough cut for the first time you have to keep in mind that the editing still has a way to go. The sound won't be adjusted. Scenes may be entirely silent because you still need music or sound effects. Many shots may just be strung together and only loosely edited because you're still not sure of the best way to use them. To an unprepared viewer it can look like a raw mess.

By the end of that first rough cut we were mentally exhausted, senses deadened and swimming in a fog. Bonnie and Michael's first comments harkened back to their initial reactions to the first draft of the script, that the party sequence had too many characters and went on too long.

Michael Dryhurst (Golden Globe-winning producer and Academy Award nominated producer for *Hope And Glory*) with Bonnie Bennett in *Year*.

I wanted *Year* to move at a brisk pace and keep ahead of the audience so over the next few weeks I cut out 51 minutes until the running time was down to 102 minutes.

One of the sections that was most heavily cut was the section that had been the hardest from the beginning of writing and through to the final editing—the New Year's Eve party sequence. In this is a part where Lana (Kristen Elizabeth) is met in an out of sight hallway by an older married man who leads her into a back bedroom where they hurriedly make love, revealing they'd been having an affair. In my drive to get the film down to a reasonable length I slashed this subplot entirely from the film, completely cutting out the performances of the two supporting actors.

This is the version that went out to festivals and was well received by audiences.

> **WARNING WHEN RUNNING ROUGH CUTS:** People cannot see into your mind, particularly regarding scenes that are not smoothed out yet. Don't base your editing decisions solely on these first reactions before you've given yourself a chance to work on the film some more.

I was proud of this version of *Year*. I also knew it could be better, and the only person who could do that was me.

Ten months passed. I wrote a script about Russian émigrés (Sacramento has one of the largest populations of Russian emigrants in the United States) and was now settling into writing the script that would become *Nightbeats*. Throughout this the party sequence in *Year* had never left my mind and I often thought about pulling out the hard drives with the *Year* footage and giving it one last try. I still had the DVD to author and thought I might be able to fix the sequence in a few hours on a day off and surprise Bonnie when she got home from work. I thought this at the time, I really thought this.

Finally one Monday morning I said to myself, "Enough thinking. Put up or shut up." I went out to the studio with the three *Year* hard drives, connected them to the Mac and clicked on the Final Cut Pro file with the film on it. And nothing was there. Oh, sure, the data and edits and references were there, but every clip had a banner that read, "Media Not Connected."

"Where is it? Two years of my life gone!"

After a dazed stupor of a few seconds it came back to me. When I'd finished cutting *Year* there were over 5,000 elements of video clips and sound effects amounting to 1.5 terabytes scattered over seven external hard drives. Before putting it into storage I'd consolidated it all onto three drives. In order to start doing any work in the Final Cut Pro file I was going to have to reconnect *all 5,000 elements.* My daydream of re-cutting the movie in a few hours evaporated in that instant. As it turned out, reconnecting all the media took nearly a week. The actual re-cutting did not begin until the following Monday.

Once I was able to sit down and finally start examining the film, opening one of the earlier longer versions of the party sequence, I was surprised to see how much really good material there was. Over the next few weeks I tinkered with the party sequence, reinstating the scenes with the two actors who had been cut out, as well as extending many of the shots by anywhere from a few frames to a quarter or half a second. Finally, the longer version worked and played smoothly, but it's pace was now completely different from the rest of the film.

One of the big bonuses of *Year* playing in the San Francisco Independent film Festival was that we got reviewed in *Variety*. Of the dozen or so dramatic films that were reviewed, *Year* was the only one to be reviewed favorably. The one criticism *Variety* did have was about the "choppy editing style." Our friend Terence Davies had similarly said that he liked most of the film very much, but found the rapid cutting style not to his particular taste. Most people commented that they liked the way the editing kept things moving. The two comments about the editing from film professionals, however, stayed on my mind.

With a fresh point of view I decided to reexamine the scenes that had particularly staccato editing. This time around I felt that *Variety*'s and Terence's criticisms were correct. It was choppy.

I chose one of these scenes where there was a series of five shots very rapidly cut together and deleted two of the shots and extended the others so that I then had a sequence of three shots that played much better. I also pulled up some of the shots that I hadn't used and inserted those in the place of others. The reedited scene now felt much truer to how I'd originally envisioned *Year* when I was writing it and, bottom line, it just looked better.

One little problem, though: the newly revised scene no longer fit in with the scenes that played before or came after it. The editing rhythms were all different. I now had to reedit those other scenes so they'd have the same pacing of fewer but longer holding shots. Once I finished reworking those scenes I found it necessary to rework the scenes that wrapped around those as well. I also put back a handful of scenes that had been deleted in order to make the film shorter, but which I now felt enhanced the story and made the movie play much better.

In the end I reexamined and adjusted every single shot of every single scene in *Year*. The simple touchup job that I imagined could be done in a few short hours on an afternoon wound up taking nearly three months.

> Making a film demands 100% commitment :
>   When starting out
>   While making it
>   In editing
>   Even after you think you've finished

There are many mainstream directors, such as Oliver Stone and Ridley Scott, who make one version of their films for the theatrical release and another for the DVD or Blu-Ray release. For a theatrical release there is enormous pressure to keep films to a certain length to get more screenings in a day and sell more tickets. Stone and Scott will also take advantage of the extra time between theatrical release to DVD release to listen to audience response and critical reactions and to rethink their movies. Oliver Stone, in addition to adding scenes for the DVD release, may even take out scenes that played in theaters because he doesn't think they work any more.

> *Year's* run time went from 102 minutes to 109 minutes, an increase of seven minutes. I gave a DVD of the new cut film to actor Blair Leatherwood, who played Brendan, Ava's husband in the film, to see how the film played for him. A few days later he e-mailed me back, "I don't know what you did but it moves so much faster now."

The Very Last Step—Desaturate, Add Contrast, Mono Audio

THE VERY LAST THING I DO ONCE THE EDITING IS ALL DONE, meaning after the rough cut and all of the edits and re-edits are finished and the film is down to the final version to send out to festivals, is I give the whole film it's final look and sound.

I export film out of Final Cut Pro. All the hundreds or thousands of takes, clips, cuts, sound and music effects are mixed down into one QuickTime clip. *Year* was 17 Gigabytes. *Nightbeats* was 12 Gigabytes.

I then import this final QuickTime clip back into Final Cut Pro and give it a color palette. Earlier I warned against shooting with filters and advised adding your look in post. This is when you do that. Either to small, individual sections or scenes, or to the entire film. I shoot my films carefully so that they are properly lit (whether with natural light or using electrical lights), exposed and color balanced.

The one consistent problem I have with cameras—whether they're DV, HD *or* the film that comes out of 16mm and 35mm cameras—is that the images they create have too much color! This was especially true of my Panasonic DVX 100A. All the footage that came out of it looked like a 1940s MGM musical. I thought Judy Garland and Mickey Rooney were going to leap out off the screen. I felt like I had to put on sunglasses because it was so vibrant and rich.

This was when I started to understand all the articles I'd read in *American Cinematographer* over the years when D.P.s would talk about "desaturation." Cameras and film stocks produce rich color. It's up to you to decide how you want to vitiate it for the end effect: use it, bleach it out, make it blue, darken it down, or get rid of it entirely and make it black & white.

Desaturating The Image

I desaturate everything 30-40%. This amount varies depending on the film. For *Year* I desaturated 33% and it looked right. I also used Final Cut Pro's effects menu and adjusted the color balance to add a very slight yellow-green tint to make it look as if the film were a memory of a year that had faded with time. For *Nightbeats* I desaturated 40% because it is a noir and the classic noirs were made in black & white. To have gone entirely to black & white would have been pretentious. I kept just enough color to keep it contemporary.

Adding Contrast

In both films I also brightened up the image by 8%, then increased contrast by 15%. This seemed to deepen the blacks and added an edge of crispness to the lines, making the images appear sharper.

Making The Audio Mono

Lots of people boast of using 5.1 Surround sound for their films, but I finish all my films with a mono track. All the sound is mixed down into two audio tracks *that are exactly the same.* This may sound old hat fashion, but it keeps me from being burned.

When Michael Dryhurst and I teamed up to make our very first experimental short film, a seven-minute comedy for the Sacramento Film Festival, I had submitted it on mini-DV with some sounds on Audio Channel One and others on Audio Channel Two so that they would come out of speakers on different sides of the theater for effect. When it was screened the projectionist had not properly connected the audio cables and only the sound from one channel of the audio was heard. A miserable, humiliating experience. Thereafter, I understood why Stanley Kubrick always released his films with a monophonic track. Even if they were advertised as being in stereophonic sound, they were two tracks that were absolutely identical to each other.

If you play in enough festivals sooner or later you can count on whatever can go wrong will go wrong with a screening: whether it's only one channel of audio being played, the image being projected in the wrong ratio, the synch being off (which is possible if the sound is going out through enough mixers and audio systems) and any number of other disasters. Even for individual screenings on DVD, you never know how good or how poor somebody's TV or sound system is. By having your sound mixed down into mono, they'll always hear the whole film.

Once You Hand Out A DVD Of Your Film—Forget About It

PEOPLE ALWAYS SAY THEY CAN'T WAIT TO SEE YOUR FILM, but once they have it in their hands it goes into a stack by the DVD player and becomes a low priority. When you hand out a DVD never expect to see it again. It's like loaning out a book, once it leaves your fingers it's history.

And never ask, "Have you watched my movie yet? What did you think?" Don't beg for compliments.

If they simply say, "Hey, I (finally) watched your movie. I liked it. It was good." What they're not telling you is, "What a piece of crap. My four year old makes better movies. Keep your day job. And don't ask me any specifics."

On the other hand if they really *do* like it they'll come up to you with a look of amazement and say, "I watched your movie and it was *really* good. You blew me away. It was just like watching a real movie. I couldn't believe you could make a movie that good for that little money. Great job. Can I buy a copy to send to my mother?" Soon more people will be asking to see your movie. That's when you'll know it works.

THE FILM IS FINISHED:
Now What?

Prepping the projection of *Nightbeats* for it's hi-def screening directly out of an Apple MacBook at The Crest Theater in Sacramento, California.

Great Expectations

WHEN YOU SET OUT MAKING A FILM YOU ALWAYS HAVE THE HIGHEST HOPES: film festivals, recognition in film magazines, getting picked up for DVD distribution and cable sales. Maybe even that rarest of chances: to be that special breakout picture that's chosen for a theatrical release.

The truth is more sobering: the overwhelming majority of films will never be seen anywhere outside of film festivals. Festivals are deluged with thousands of entries every year. The 2008 Sundance Film Festival received over 9,000 entries for only a handful of positions.

The vast majority of first-time D.I.Y. filmmakers need to embark on their filmmaking venture with the understanding that it's very likely their family and friends will be the only audience to ever see their film.

Sending Your Baby Out

Your film is finished and ready to go out to the world. Despite the obstacles facing you getting into film festivals, they are still the best first stop because being played in film festivals usually *is* the theatrical release for D.I.Y. no-budget films.

Make sure you haven't blown all of your money and credit on making the film. It costs to submit to festivals, an average of $40 to $75 for each entry. The more fests you submit to the more it will cost. But it's like playing the lottery: you don't put your money down, you don't stand a chance at anything.

Start with the big festivals first: Sundance, Toronto, Tribeca, Raindance, Los Angeles, San Francisco, London, Austin. Be forewarned: these are *incredibly* hard to get into. All over the world thousands of people with camcorders and computer editing are doing the same thing as you and they all submit to the big name fests.

Most of the big festivals insist on being the world premiere venue for the films they run. Don't shoot your film in the foot by submitting to smaller festivals first.

And don't tell people what festivals you submit to. Many people broadcast that they've sent their baby off to Sundance and then are devastated when they get their rejection e-mail.

Only announce the festivals that you're accepted into—*not* the ones you aren't.

Finding The Best Venue—Niche Festivals

Once you've made the rounds with the high-profile festivals (and hopefully you managed to get in), start narrowing your focus and strategizing which festivals may be best for your film and for gaining exposure for you as a filmmaker.

Depending on the genre of your film some festivals are better suited than others. There are festivals devoted exclusively to short subjects, documentary, horror, cowboys, gay and lesbian, Jewish, Christian, women's issues, family, children, student, Italian, French, African-American, Latin or Hispanic, Native American, Asian, animation, technology, independent, D.I.Y., digital, wildlife, hiking, biking and sailing just to name a few. If there's a subject that people with camcorders are making films about there's a festival for it.

Every genre has websites devoted to it, which can be helpful to find a festival that you can try and get your film into.

Just because your film doesn't get accepted into the festival of your dreams, keep in mind that *Swingers* didn't make it into Sundance and it is now regarded as a classic comedy.

Start narrowing your festival target.

It's better to have your film play in a festival—*any* festival— than to never get played at all.

Get Your Press Kit Together

IF YOU'VE FOLLOWED MY RECOMMENDATION at the beginning of the book and registered your name as a domain name and been slowly building a website about you and your film, posting blog updates throughout the production with photos, behind-the-scenes video clips, scenes and a trailer, then you should have a fully developed site by now and be in excellent shape. If you haven't got a site going yet and you thought making the movie was a lot of work, then I hate to tell you but you're only at the eighteen mile-marker of this marathon. Time to get cracking.

Once you've finished the editing you feel physically and mentally wrung out—from the writing, the shooting, the editing, the re-editing, and then, yes, *more editing*. Call the film "done" and give yourself a well-earned break. For about a week. By then, if not already, you should be investigating film festivals to submit to.

Register your film with Withoutabox (withoutabox.com). This is an online submission site that is registered with virtually every film festival on the planet. You pay a fee of around $100 to register your film, fill out the info on it—short, narrative feature, running length, synopsis, language of origin, screening format, etc.—then you never have to fill out another entry form. Every day you'll receive a list of festivals that are accepting entries and others that are near their final deadlines. There's background info on the festivals and links to their websites so you can find the festivals that could be good for you and your film. Then it's as simple as making a few clicks of the mouse, "Qualify for this festival" and "Submit," pay the entry fees, seal the DVDs in envelopes, address, stamp and put your baby in the mail. Then the gut twisting begins. You wait. And wait. And wait.

Submission deadlines are typically three to six months before the festival takes place. The best thing to do during this time is to simply forget about it. Good festivals get thousands of submissions. The competition is incredibly high. Don't develop an ulcer over it. Eventually, just when you start to think the post office lost your entry, you get an e-mail informing you that your film is either "in" or "out."

If your film is lucky enough to be accepted, a whole new mountain of work now awaits you.

When you submitted your film no press kit was required. As soon as your film is accepted everything changes. All of a sudden you need a press kit with:

- Production information
- Cast and crew credits
- JPEG's of scenes from the film and behind-the-scenes
- Story synopsis
- Filmmaker FAQ
- A poster of the film for display at the theater and on the festival website.

In the past all this had to be submitted on paper with a CD-ROM, which invariably got lost and a reporter would call desperately at the last minute asking for a new one to be FedExed. Today this is all posted from your film website. Journalists simply cut and paste copy directly from your site into their articles. I've even had reporters from major newspapers ask me for a quote, and rather than do an interview will simply e-mail a list of questions for me to write my responses and e-mail them back.

Filmmaker FAQ

This is a self-conducted interview. We've all read interviews with filmmakers and imagined how we'd handle our own interviews. A filmmaker FAQ is exactly that, a series of frequently asked questions you anticipate a journalist would ask: "How did you get the idea for your film?" "How difficult was it to make?" "Where did you find your actors?" "Why did it take you two years to finish?" And on and on, to which you provide your own perfectly worded answers.

A Great Poster & 4"x6" Handout Cards

Hopefully you've spent some of your downtime since sending your movie off to festivals by working on a poster. I had not done that on *Year*, then had to make a mad rush to get my entire press kit together and design a poster from scratch in just a matter of weeks. Now I'll spend months developing a poster and trying many graphic styles and arrangements before settling on the final version.

A word of advice: design your poster in small pieces over time. It takes a while to get the small things right. At a festival people will decide whether they want to see your film or not based on how cool the poster is.

The poster is what goes on the front of 4"x6" film cards. You find stacks of these at festivals for every film playing, just as you'll find similar cards at record stores promoting local musicians and independent CDs. Success at a festival depends on how many people you can pack into the screening of your film. The festival is running your film but it's up to you to promote it. Have 500 or a thousand cards printed up for your screening and put a stack in the theater lobby (or lobbies if there are multiple screening venues), at coffee shops and clubs in the area, record stores, book stores, video stores, any place you can think of to attract an audience.

Producer-actor Bonnie Bennett with our poster outside The Roxie Theater at the San Francisco Independent Film Festival.

Filmcards are printed on sturdy stock and double-sided. The front promotes the film, the back promotes you, the filmmaker. Select the best behind-the-scenes photo(s) of you shooting the movie, then include your name, website and e-mail contact. Leave off any addresses or phone numbers. Make your card as cool as possible. When I attend festivals I pick up cards for all the films playing to study their graphics and look for better ways to make mine stand out. These are also impressive to hand out as business cards.

Youtube & The World

Even filmmaking giants like Francis Ford Coppola and David Lynch have turned to Youtube to post trailers and video clips of their latest film projects rather than using more traditionally established media. YouTube goes out to an enormous worldwide audience and is completely free to use. No small thing to be overlooked even by world-renowned artists like Coppola and Lynch.

The ultimate test for your movie is to be able to attract complete strangers to want to see your work. This couple was looking for a movie to see that night, liked the poster for *Year* and bought a ticket. After the film they told me that they had no idea what they were going to see, but were glad they'd come to see *this* film.

EARLY CONCEPT POSTER FOR *NIGHTBEATS*. The inspiration for the multiple images of Lori Foxworth as Mercy was drawn from John Cassavetes' poster for *A Woman Under The Influence,* which featured a similar repetition photographs of Gena Rowlands.

A FEW VERSIONS LATER. Trying to find a cleaner, more sophisticated concept. Changing the main image of Mercy to this one showing her as a pole dancer adds clarity to both who she is and reinforces the noir aspect of the story. Also note how the streamlining of the credits simplifies the graphics. Actor-writer Anthony D'Juan encouraged me to combine the credits to "A Mike Carroll Film."

FINAL VERSION. Greatly scaled down, using the power of minimalism to sell the essentials.

Mainstream Hollywood movie posters are dominated by big face close-ups of stars. If it's a romantic comedy they're smiling, an action film they're grimacing, a drama they're serious. More than anything, big studio movies are sold by well-known stars with proven track records.

D.I.Y. filmmakers don't have stars so we have to sell the film itself. Keep the graphics of the poster simple. Don't rely on the faces of your actors because they're unknown. And don't clutter it up with a lot of credits. Everyone's got a credit at the end of the movie. A poster is not a vanity page to show off you and everybody who worked on it. Leave that for your website and Facebook.

A poster is advertising. Its sole purpose is to get people who don't know anything about your film to want to see it.

BACK SIDE OF THE 4x6 HANDOUT CARD. The front of the card, the A-Side, should be the official poster of your film. With the B-Side it's important to let people know when and where it's being screened.

Film festivals are showcases for new filmmakers so it's important to promote yourself. Include a behind-the-scenes photo of you actively making the film. Print your name in bold lettering followed by the various job titles you performed and an e-mail address in case someone with a lot of disposable cash wants to contact you.

Since the poster had been streamlined so much I used the B-Side for the row of actors' photos to promote them as well. All their images are taken from frames of the film. This is something Stanley Kubrick did as opposed to using photos taken by an on-set photographer. I selected frames that best represented the characters they are playing.

Online printing companies will make 500 double-sided 4x6 handout cards for around $50. It may sound like one more added expense but getting into a festival is so hard that you need to promote every screening you can. Believe me, there's nothing more depressing than having your movie play on a big screen to just five people.

Film family at the premiere of *Nightbeats* in the Sacramento Film & Music Festival at the fabulous Crest Theater. Lori Foxworth, Mike & Bonnie Carroll and daughter/"critic" Jenna Lincoln.

Make Sure Your Film Is Screened Your Way

THE 2006 SAN FRANCISCO INDEPENDENT FILM FESTIVAl screened films on 35mm, 16mm and DVCAM. *Year* was digital so I would have been insane to spend $20,000 for a blowup to film. I rented a DVCAM deck for a weekend, bought three 120 minute tapes and printed out three copies of *Year*, then proofed them watching every frame. After a year and a half of editing the film, having to sit through it three more times in the same day was a major effort, but the last thing you want at a screening is for the tape to be wrinkled, the picture to freeze up or the sound to drop out.

One tape was mailed off to Indiefest, one I carried in my coat pocket to the screenings in case their copy became inexplicably lost (which didn't happen) and the third was kept in my car in a nearby parking lot as an added redundancy. Naturally, having covered all my bases, the film played without a hitch.

While participating in S.F. Independent we got a call informing us that *Year* had been accepted into a festival in Los Angeles.

"Wow, that's great," I thanked the woman. "What format do you want for the screening?"

"Oh, that won't matter. The DVD you sent with your festival entry is fine."

"A DVD? Really? Wouldn't you want something higher quality for projecting on a big screen?"

"It's really no problem, most of the other films are running from DVDs. Your submission copy will be fine."

This made me nervous. The last thing I wanted was to have *Year* look like some crappy camcorder video in the motion picture capital of the world.

> TECHNICAL NOTE: *Year* ran 102 minutes (in festivals, prior to re-cutting it for DVD). As a self-contained QuickTime file this was 17 Gigabytes. The full, uncompressed version was transferred to DVCAM cassette for the San Francisco Independent Film Festival and looked fabulous on a thirty foot screen. A single-layer DVD only holds 4.5 Gigabytes, playing a highly compressed file that is only one-quarter to one-fifth of the file size. On a big screen that results in significant picture loss.

Bonnie and I drove down to Los Angeles with great excitement. *Year* was playing at five o'clock on a Friday. When we arrived the lobby was empty. We went up to the screening room and there were five people in the audience. It turned out they were the makers of the films that had run before us. We were also joined by Dominick Bernal, who had helped with the sound on the party scene, and Francesca "Kitten" Natividad, a friend and actor who conveniently happened to live around the corner from the festival.

The film got under way. And it looked terrible. It was playing off a DVD onto a twenty-foot wide screen and

Francesca "Kitten" Natividad, iconic Russ Meyer ultravixen, liked Mike and Bonnie's first film *Year* and was happy to sign onto *Nightbeats*.

looked soft, washed out and flat. Then, to add salt to the wound, three-quarters of the way in the DVD locked up and the picture froze. I had a back-up DVD in my pocket and went scrambling to the projection room where the projectionist, a young kid, wasn't even monitoring the screening. He led me to the DVD player and after a moment or two of fiddling there was nothing to do except fast forward ahead a minute and let the film continue from there and pray that it didn't freeze up again. Luckily, the rest of the movie ran without difficulty for the handful of us there.

Up to this screening I always said that a filmmaker should be grateful if just one person shows up to see their movie. This screening put that to the test.

We left the screening and, as polite as I was to everyone there, I was seething inside. When I'd gone into the projection room to correct the freeze frame situation I'd discovered that on the shelf directly beneath the DVD player was a DVCAM deck—the very same format deck that had so stunningly run *Year* in San Francisco just a month before. The organizer who was putting on the festival was only involved in the selection of the films and the administration of the festival and had no clue about the technical aspects of projection.

A few months later *Year* played in a festival in Sacramento. I didn't want any problems at this screening so I said that I'd provide a DVCPRO playback deck and play the film off a high-resolution DVCPRO cassette. All I needed to know was whether the projector could project in 16:9 widescreen or should I make a letterboxed 4:3 version?

"No, no, 16:9 is fine."

"Really? You're sure? Your projector plays 16:9?"

"Oh, yeah, sure."

"Okay, so I don't have to worry about letterboxing?"

"No, no. We're good."

The night of the screening I brought the DVCPRO playback deck and the 16:9 version on a DVCPRO tape. It was a cold, rainy night, yet a crowd of over 120 people turned out for the express purpose of seeing our film. We didn't start running until after ten o'clock and when it started projecting on the screen the picture was a squeezed 4:3, not widescreen 16:9. I went tearing backstage and had the projectionist halt the film.

"Why? What's the matter? It looks great."

"It's square."

"Yeah."

"It's supposed to be 16x9."

"Yeah."

"That means it's widescreen—rectangular. You're running it square."

The projectionist just stared back at me blankly. He had no idea what 16:9 was.

I frantically checked the menu of the projector and found there wasn't a setting for 16:9. It was an older model made before media started to be produced in 16:9. There was nothing to do but let the film play as it was, looking like one of those old Twentieth Century-Fox CinemaScope films on TV with credits playing in squeezed anamorphic and all the people looking like they're ten feet tall and pipe-cleaner thin.

Blair Leatherwood was in the back of the auditorium and I went up to him, mortified. "I'm sorry about this. Tonight everybody looses twenty pounds."

"What do you mean? I think it looks great."

In the end, I'm not sure how many people noticed. No one walked out and there were tears and laughter in all the right places. Based on the audience response it was still a successful screening and several people wanted to know when they could buy the DVD, which made me resolve to always have DVDs whenever one of my films was screened from then on.

D.I.Y. Film—D.I.Y. Projection

NIGHTBEATS HAD IT'S FIRST SCREENING before a hometown audience in the 2010 Sacramento Film & Music Festival at The Crest Theater, a fabulous old movie house with a huge screen in a thousand-seat auditorium. After having a variety of experiences with projection at festivals I decided to take more control over any future screenings. *Nightbeats* had been shot in 720 HDV and I wanted to preserve the high-resolution picture that a screening in standard definition simply could not come close to. Determined to stay true to my D.I.Y. roots I played *Nightbeats* directly out of my MacBook. This way I could preserve every pixel and byte from the QuickTime 12 Gigabyte clip and get the highest quality image on the screen. All that was needed was a DVI adapter cable to connect from the projector port on the side of the MacBook. The audio was as simple as plugging in audio cables to the Mac's stereo headphone jack.

I tested my plan days before the screening to make absolutely sure it would work and it came off without a hitch. Confident as I was, though, I still carried a DVD in my pocket just in case.

On the afternoon of the screening I was at The Crest by four, hooked the MacBook up to the projector and audio system, did a picture and sound level check and all systems were "Go." It was then a long couple of hours before the audience settled into their seats, the film was introduced and the lights dimmed. I tapped the MacBook's space bar, QuickTime started to play. "The Garage Filmworks" title projected onto the same epic screen where just a few years before I'd seen a reissue of *The Bridge On The River Kwai.* Jimmy Bell's sound design poured out the theater speakers and *Nightbeats* was playing.

To keep the laptop out of the audience's view I'd set it on the seat of a folding chair next to the projector with a black T-shirt draped over the screen. I sat next to it with my legs stretched out on either side of the chair for the first few minutes to make sure the film was playing perfectly before planning on heading up into the audience to join Bonnie, Lori and co-star Kelly Patton Nixon. About then someone walked behind me in the shadows and I suddenly realized how dark the theater was. It was so dark that people could be going by without ever seeing me. And if they couldn't see me then they also couldn't see the laptop with the black T-shirt covered over it. One accidental bump in the dark and the whole movie premiere would come crashing to a halt. It was so pitch black that I couldn't see my feet nor any of the cables coming out of the laptop. If I moved I ran the risk of pulling out the AC power cable or DVI video cable or stereo audio cable. This left me with only one option: I had to remain sitting exactly as I was and do absolutely nothing, not even move my feet so much as an inch, for the full 89 minutes of the movie.

In spite of that mild inconvenience, the movie played flawlessly. The picture was pristine. The sound was rich and layered and filled the auditorium. The audience reacted with laughter or gasps at exactly the right moments. The rest of the time you could hear a pin drop. When the credits rolled the audience broke out into applause.

There's always a huge question mark when you start a film: "Will I be able to pull it off?" In the case of *Nightbeats* it meant telling a story in a genre, noir, that I had neither worked in nor contemplated before. It also meant raising the bar visually and technically by shooting HDV and at night, as well as figuring out how to light the night scenes and maintain my cinematographer's aesthetic of not wanting them to look like they're lit at all. As well as taking on a collaborator in Jimmy Bell to design a multilayered soundscape for the ear.

In the end, the film played without a hitch and exactly on my own terms.

Avoid The Sharks: D.I.Y. Film—D.I.Y Distribution

MOST INDIE FILMMAKERS' IDEA OF A DISTRIBUTION DEAL is to be picked up for an art house theatrical release, accompanied by a check that will reimburse their production costs and maybe a nice little profit.

Let's be very clear: *This doesn't happen.*

This may have been the case in decades past but in today's environment where the digital revolution has made it affordable for anybody to make a film, which has produced a population explosion of independent and D.I.Y. Films allowing distributors to take their pick without having to put up a penny.

A much more likely scenario is that a distributor may offer a partnership arrangement. If any money is offered it will be at the very most a few thousand dollars.

If theatrical distribution in independent art houses is being offered there will most likely need to be considerable monies spent for a post-production audio mix and a 35mm or HD transfer. The current conversion of theaters to digital projection may help to bring down these post costs. Add to that the costs involved in any marketing and advertising to be done. Indie art house releases are hitting fewer and fewer cities and taking in less and less box office. A pay-per-view and DVD release will be necessary to cover distribution costs. The distributor should already have relationships with companies in these areas making these venues easier to break into. As a practical matter, since the distributor is covering all these costs they will insist on getting their investment back first. It's not uncommon that a distribution deal may require signing over all business decisions on your film for ten to twenty years.

Let me repeat: The distributor will control your film for 10 to 20 years.

Any money you see will only be after *their* costs have been recouped and on a 50-50 or smaller percentage split. In other words, *forget it.*

Most indie flicks' life after film festivals is *only* on DVD. Here again, a distributor can be helpful in getting your film out onto shelves and the costs will be drastically less than getting it out to theaters, though there will still be costs that the distributor will be entitled to recoup before you ever see a penny.

- D.I.Y. films almost never play on any movie screens outside of festivals.
- Some filmmakers have had some success by "four-walling" their film—renting a cinema and screening it themselves to target niche audiences.
- It is the incredibly rare film that gets picked up for a theatrical release. In that case, don't call them—they'll call you.

Year premiered in the 2006 San Francisco Independent Film Festival, a two-week festival presenting films by prestigious filmmakers from Australia, Hong Kong, Taiwan, Japan and South Korea to people like me making films with camcorders and credit cards.

Within six months the titles from the festival started showing up on the DVD shelves of my neighborhood video store. I'd look on the back of the DVD boxes to find out who was distributing these films and, in most cases, the filmmakers were distributing their films themselves. Of course, the film needs to stand out in a catalogue so that a video storeowner will want to buy it. "This is something my customers will want to rent."

Self-distribution and on-line downloads are new opportunities that more and more beginning filmmakers are turning to. Don't even think about burning the disks yourself. DVD duplication machines are getting cheaper, but the cost of ink alone is not going to make it worth all your time and effort. You're also going to need an ISBN number and bar code. Amazon, Blockbuster, even independent video stores require an ISBN number and bar code for their inventory systems. A DVD duplication company or self-publishing organization (I've used DiscMakers.com and CreateSpace.com) will provide the ISBN number and bar code for you and even have templates indicating where they will go on your disks and box art so you can design around them. You can have a thousand DVDs duplicated with graphics printed on the disk, in a box with a full-color jacket that includes a bar-code for a thousand bucks or less.

A big advantage to using CreateSpace's self-publishing is that the DVD of your film, CD or book is sold directly from Amazon.com, the biggest and best department store in the world.

I'll never forget when the VHS market was taking off back in the 80s and my friend Russ Meyer was putting all of his Bosomania collection (*Faster, Pussycat! Kill! Kill!*, *Vixen*, *Beneath The Valley Of The Ultravixen* to name a few) out on tape. He could get a hundred copies made with labels on the cassette, box art printed and shrink-wrapped for $1.99 each, which he then sold himself out of his house for $89.95

each. He told me this, then started laughing.

"What's so funny?" I asked him.

"That's what I sound like when I'm going to the bank."

- Develop a website to promote and market your film(s).
- Spread the word via free-to-use social networking groups like Facebook and Twitter (and whatever else may pop up next week).
- Sell your movies off your own site out of your own house. Eliminate the middleman and overhead.

This may be the best, if not the only way for the D.I.Y. filmmaker creating movies for $5,000 to $30,000 or so to *ever* see a nickel. It won't make you rich but it may help get your film seen, your talents known and your next film made.

The vast majority of movies, including Hollywood blockbusters, reach their largest audiences through DVD sales and rentals. Get your film on DVD and you'll be in good company.

Getting Your Films Out On Your Terms

ANOTHER WAY TO GET YOUR FILM OUT to the cinema-going public is through self-distribution to independent movie theaters. In the past this was always a financially prohibitive option requiring a 35mm blowup, multiple prints struck and pounding the pavement to find independent theater owners who'd run your film. The new wave of digital projection systems being installed in independent movie houses could change that ball game entirely. All that's needed now is to have a film that can attract enough of an audience for a movie house to be able to sell tickets and you could be in business.

This may sound like an over simplification but digital delivery and projection is going to make the serious independent and D.I.Y. filmmaker rethink their work into more commercial terms. I don't mean simply splashing hot booty and shootouts across the screen, but to consider how to make whatever you are working on so that it is compelling and can reach out and pull in an audience.

We can't compete against the studios on their blockbuster terms, but we may be able to go under the radar and survive, and maybe even thrive, while making the kinds of films that we want to make by creating relationships with the independent cinemas, as well as putting our films out on DVD ourselves. Times have changed and nobody knows where we are going to be in even five years from now. The filmmakers who succeed are going to be the ones who see the doors opening and step through them ahead of everyone else.

There are many people who call themselves artists, but for me an artist is someone with a vision who tells their own stories on their own terms. It may not necessarily be a journey that I am going to enjoy every step of the way, but if the artist is truly original then I'll trust them enough to go along for the ride.

John Cassavetes—American Independent

John Cassavetes' films are a marvel in their simplicity. Anything but mainstream and completely uncompromising. The filmmaking techniques are sometimes crude and the sound could often be better, but they are absolute testaments to honest storytelling and performances.

Cassavetes was totally independent. He wouldn't waste time looking for funding, which has become the mantra of today's independent film movement. His motivation for acting in TV and movies was to earn enough to be free to make his own films his own way with his own cash.

Most people in Hollywood thought he was eccentric or crazy, making a little 16mm black and white movie up at his house in the hills at night and on weekends. They also thought he was nuts spending two years editing it in his garage. After a few test screenings in some film festivals, he convinced a small Hollywood art house cinema to book his "crazy" movie. *Faces* (1968) played there for a year and earned Academy Award nominations for Best Supporting Actor for Seymour Cassel, Best Supporting Actress for Lynn Carlin, and for John Cassavetes for Best Original Screenplay.

Cassavetes owned his films outright and distributed them himself by looking through newspapers of cities across the country for theaters running movies like his, then picking up the phone and calling the owners directly to arrange his own bookings.

A few years later he put these methods to the test once more with *A Woman Under The Influence* (1974), regarded as his masterpiece. Again self-financed by Cassavetes, his wife Gena Rowlands and co-star Peter Falk, the film was shot in a rented house with a crew of students from the American Film Institute (A.F.I.) and volunteers who Cassavetes trained himself. The typical studio-produced movie of that time would shoot between 100,000 and 200,000 feet of 35mm film. (Film runs through a 35mm projector at a rate of 5,000 feet per hour.) On *A Woman Under The Influence*, Cassavetes shot one million feet, or 200 hours of film, which took another two years to edit.

He then picked up the phone and booked *Woman* at the same cinemas that had run *Faces* with so much success, as well as other cinemas that were doing very well at the time with foreign films. Over the course of the next year *A Woman Under The Influence* would receive Oscar nominations for Best Actress for Gena Rowlands and Best Director for John Cassavetes, the highest recognition that a self-financed, totally independent film had ever received, and earned over

$10 million at the box office.

David Lynch & The Filmless Future

Just as John Cassavetes is credited with inventing the American independent filmmaker model in the 1960s and '70s, David Lynch is establishing the new digital independent model for the 21st Century.

After *Mulholland Drive* (2001) Lynch, who had been a mystery man from the moment he first set foot in Los Angles, mystified everyone even more when he simply turned his back and walked away from the Hollywood system. Lynch had an extremely loyal fan base, but was faced with escalating production costs and increasing limitations imposed by the studios.

Lynch was one of the first artists to recognize the potential in the Internet as more than merely a means of instant communication, but as a distribution device for digital entertainment. He was also one the first people to realize that he was his own greatest commodity and became one of the first individuals to register their name as a website, davidlynch.com. By eliminating not only the middleman but the production system as well, Lynch became completely unleashed. He was free to create his own short films and animations, without oversight and restrictions, and deliver them directly to his media-savvy fan base via his website on a monthly subscription basis, with all the proceeds going directly back into his own pocket.

A few years later he bought two Sony PD-150 mini-DV camcorders and started experimenting with video. As a student Lynch had a writing instructor who taught that all you need are seventy scenes and you've got a movie. Lynch applied that fractured, interwoven tapestry of vignette storytelling to *Inland Empire* (2006), his first feature film since leaving the studios.

I saw *Inland Empire* in a tiny art house theater with a soft print and even softer focus. Within minutes I knew this 160-minute film was going to be a long and rough ride. By the time it was over my head was splitting and I was in dire need of cabernet. I also knew that I'd just witnessed genius.

Laura Dern plays a film actress playing many different characters in a film-within-a-film, which blurs reality and madness. After a while you're no longer certain if you're watching the film she's making or if it's all a figment of the imagination of someone who is floating on the edge of madness. It's totally raw, unrestrained, unglamorous and a horror masterwork.

The DVD includes a 30-minute documentary showing David Lynch at work making the film in much the same way that I work as a one-man filmmaker. Lynch shot most of his digital opus himself with Sony PD-150 camcorders set on "auto," meaning the exposure, audio, white balance and focus were on automatic settings. He did his own editing and sound design (nobody creates mood sounds better than David Lynch) on his Mac in Final Cut.

It's inspiring and empowering to see a world-renowned iconoclast and creator of classic motion pictures, such as *Blue Velvet, The Elephant Man* and the TV series *Twin Peaks,* now charting his own course on his own terms and with cameras, computers and software that are available to the public online or at electronics stores. Certainly if predecessors like Orson Welles and John Cassavetes were still with us today they would be exploring the digital terrain and creating their work available that their audiences could access online without the middlemen.

What Now?

THE OLD ADAGE, "TRUTH IS BEAUTY," should also include an asterisk leading to another adage, "Truth Can Be Painful." The hard, rock-bottom honest truth to the vast, vast majority of D.I.Y. no-budget filmmakers out there is this: The reason so many thousands of your films didn't make it into the festivals you wanted, or any festivals at all, is that they just weren't good enough.

Galen Howard feels the lure of the night in *Nightbeats*.

All right, that was the sugarcoated explanation. Here's the real unglossed, untouched, give-it-to-me-I-can-take-it answer. Get a grip first. Take a shot of cabernet or bourbon or rotgut or whatever you need to get you through.

The Absolute Bottom Line Don't-Be-Nice-Be-Honest reason why your film didn't get anywhere: Because it wasn't any good. It was crap. A 90-minute home movie. Plain and simple. You may not be able to accept that at the moment. Understood. You've worked body and soul for a long time. I'm sorry to be the bearer of bad news, but the God's honest truth is that not everybody (in fact, incredibly few) can hit one out of the park their first time up to bat. It takes time and practice

Do yourself a favor: forget about it for a while. Put your movie in a drawer. Go get reacquainted with the family or whoever. Mow the lawn. Get out of town. Go fishing. Go to the beach. Go to the desert. Go to the mountains. Treat yourself for a while. You've earned it.

In a few months or a year take the movie out and watch it again. Be honest with yourself. How does it really look? Maybe it's worth fixing. Re-cut it. Maybe this 90-minute comedy that nobody's laughing at could work at twenty minutes, or fifteen, or ten? It's a lot easier to get a short into a festival than a feature. And the entry fees for shorts are cheaper.

Another option is to post your film on line. There are lots of sites where independent filmmakers can post full-length films. If you weren't able to get into a festival at least this is one way for people to see your movie.

Or maybe your movie should just go back in the drawer. A learning experience. You always dreamed of making a movie. You got it out of your system. At least you had the guts to try. Most people don't even do that much. Life goes on. Move on with it. Go on eBay, sell your camera, lights and whatever else and pay off that credit card or go on that trip to Europe you always dreamed of. Check another dream off the list.

Or maybe you realize now what you should have done. You tried too big. You need to get smaller and more intimate.

If you made your movie before you read this book maybe now you're thinking that you want to take another stab at it. Only without so many people around telling you what you should be doing.

Or maybe you know how to make that same movie all over again and a lot better. Why not? You've got the camera. You've got the computer. You've got the tapes or memory cards or whatever media your camera records onto. Do it. Practice makes perfect. Or, if not "perfect," perhaps "improved."

That's It For Now

That's my soapbox. With any luck the sequel to this book will be *Ten Man Strike Team: How To Make A Million Dollar Movie Look Like A Blockbuster*. But I'm not holding my breath.

I've tried to pass along what works for me. Use what you want. Make the best movie you can. When you've finished, send me a DVD. I'd like to see how it worked out.

And remember, whatever you want to do, nobody's going to do it for you.

In the meantime, don't quit your day job.

Films You Can Learn From

Wonderland (U.K., 1999. Dir: Michael Winterbottom, D.P. Sean Bobbitt)

This is one of my all-time favorite films, along with *Lawrence of Arabia* and *War And Peace* (1967, U.S.S.R, dir: Sergei Bondarchuk). A simple story following four days in the lives of a working-class family in London. One of the most beautifully shot films I've ever seen, done with handheld 16mm cameras in documentary-style. The only lighting in the film was accomplished by replacing regular light bulbs with color-corrected photofloods. And an epic, symphonic score by Michael Nyman. This film was a tremendous influence on my filmmaking style for *Year*. The performances are completely invisible.

The Manchurian Candidate, Seven Days In May, The Train, Seconds, French Connection II, The Gypsy Moths, Ronin, Andersonville, Reindeer Games (U.S.A., Dir: John Frankenheimer)

Some of these are classics, others are well intentioned, but all were directed by John Frankenheimer and the DVDs include his audio commentaries, which are detailed, impassioned, candid and insightful on the down-in-the-trenches grunt work of moviemaking. I keep his audio commentaries on my iPod and replay one every few months.

Fail Safe, Dog Day Afternoon, Network, The Morning After, The Verdict, Night Falls On Manhattan, Before The Devil Knows You're Dead (U.S.A., dir: Sidney Lumet)

Sidney Lumet has made more classic American films than any director I can think of: *12 Angry Men, Long Day's Journey Into Night, The Pawnbroker, Fail Safe, Serpico, Dog Day Afternoon, Network, Prince Of The City, The Verdict*—and that's leaving out a lot.

The titles at the top of this section are all available on DVD with his audio commentary, which are master classes in filmmaking. His knowledge of lenses is precise, but the greatest lesson to be drawn from Lumet's commentaries is how much he values actors. On the DVD of *Night Falls On Manhattan* there's a second audio commentary with several of the lead actors discussing working with Lumet, which is revelatory. You can learn more about how to work with and direct actors from listening to Lumet's audio commentary than you will ever get from any directing class. (Unless you take one of mine.)

With his courtroom TV series *100 Centre Street* he made the transition from film to HD 24p filmmaking and never looked back. *Before The Devil Knows You're Dead* is a masterful film and shows that whatever can be done on 35mm can be just as beautiful in HD.

Italian For Beginners (2000, Denmark, dir: Lone Scherfig)

A simply done romantic comedy-drama from the Danish film collective Dogme 95. Shot on camcorders with no lighting or tripods, with all the sound recorded live and no post production ADR. It was at the top of critics' lists when it was released in the U.S. and in Denmark is one of the most successful films of all time. An amazing example of what can be done with a good script, good actors, and honest filmmaking. The type of film that this book is all about and that anyone with a good idea and basic technical knowledge is capable of making.

Coming Home (U.S.A., 1978, dir: Hal Ashby)

Starring Jane Fonda, Jon Voight, Bruce Dern.

Aside from being a great film, I suggest this as a study in lighting. I like films that look as close to the real world as possible and disguise whatever additional lighting has been used. In the audio commentary cinematographer Haskell Wexler discusses his use of soft lighting, bounce cards, handheld and telephoto shooting to convey an honest, documentary-style sense of authenticity. There is also considerable discussion by actors Jon Voight and and Bruce Dern of the working methods of director Hal Ashby, regarded as one of the great filmmakers of the 70s. The editing style of director Hal Ashby is a study in how to blend music to tell story in lieu of dialogue.

Bullitt—The Special Edition (U.S.A., 1968, dir: Peter Yates)

As much as I love this Steve McQueen movie, the best part of this disk is the DVD Extra: a 90-minute documentary *The Cutting Edge: The Magic Of Movie Editing*. This is appropriate since *Bullitt* won the 1968 Academy Award for Best Editing. *The Cutting Edge* chronicles the history of film editing and includes interviews with the best film editors in the business. Crappy movies are cut technically. The best movies are edited based on gut instinct and emotional reaction to the material. Another must-have DVD. Not to be rented, but added to your library.

Venus (U.K., 2007, dir: Roger Mitchell)

A contemporary gem. Perhaps a quiet masterpiece. Starring Peter O'Toole in a study-in-acting performance as an actor at the end of his days, who still has the passion of life burning in him.

The cinematography is simple, yet eye-catching. Locations are real. Many of the exterior scenes were shot on actual streets and sidewalks without any crowd control, using wireless mics on the actors and filming with existing light using hidden cameras and strong telephoto lenses so as not to draw attention.

The interior scenes are lit eloquently and minimally, employing small lights that could be plugged into ordinary wall sockets and requiring no big generators that the soundman had to work around.

Venus is a study in simple, clear, efficient and contemporary storytelling and filmmaking.

The Duelists (U.K., 1976, dir: Ridley Scott)

Aside from being a visually stunning film, Ridley Scott gives one of the best audio commentaries I've ever heard on how to make a film with very little money, creative use of locations, using his crew members for extras, and the timesaving benefits of being his own camera operator. It's like listening to an audio book memoir. I keep this loaded on my iPod and listen to it about once a month.

Trainspotting, 28 Days Later, Millions, Sunshine, Slumdog Millionaire (U.K., Danny Boyle)

Any film that Danny Boyle makes is worth your time. There is so much energy and passion in every frame, and this comes across in his audio commentaries. When you listen to him talk about his films you can immediately understand why he's such a successful filmmaker. When he speaks he throws himself body and soul into every sentence, emphatically punctuating his words in the most dynamic of ways.

I can't help but imagine that if I was a studio executive and Danny Boyle was sitting across from me, using all of his exuberance and zeal to describe the next film he wanted to make, I could not help but find myself irresistibly pounding the table and shouting out, "Yes! I want to see that movie! Let's do it!"

As filmmakers we have to be passionate about our films in order to get other people excited enough to want to make them want to work with us and to get others to want to see our movies and buy them on DVD. People want to be transported when they see a movie and listening to Danny Boyle talk about his movies makes you want to go on the journey with him.

Lake of Fire (2006, dir: Tony Kaye)

Tony Kaye, director-cinematographer-camera operator-editor, established himself making commercials and music videos before entering the feature filmmaking maelstrom with *American History X*. His goal was to not simply make a competent first film, he wanted to make one of the best films ever made. His first cut was 85 minutes and got tremendous audience response. However, the film's star Edward Norton felt it was not performance-driven enough and used his star-status to reedit the film to 119 minutes. This version also earned excellent reviews and a Best Actor Oscar Nomination for Norton. It's a powerful film and one can only wonder what Tony Kaye's cut looked like. Perhaps with the alternate versions of films being released on DVD we may someday get the privilege to see.

For several years Kaye's feature filmmaking seemed lost in the wilderness, then in 2007 he reemerged with *Lake of Fire*, a documentary that he'd been working on, amazingly, for over twenty years.

Kaye moved from Britain to the United States in the 1980s. Coming from a socialized country where abortion had been legal for some time he was fascinated by the religious wars raging around the abortion issue and the protests at Planned Parenthood clinics. He decided to explore this subject as a film and spent years traveling around the country filming events with his own 35mm motion picture camera in black and white, funding all of this out of his own pocket. He was able to gain access to everybody, extremists as well as women going to clinics to have their procedures. Kaye's camera is unsparing and blindingly honest. He doesn't censor anything for the comfort of the viewer.

The project eventually spanned two decades, starting in 35mm, then to Super-16mm, finally HD, at a reported personal cost of over $5 million. The film was completed in HD and started screening at film festivals in HD in 2006. If the film had gone into general release it would have certainly received an NC-17 rating. He shows the clinical operations as well as graphic crime scene photographs of doctors who've been murdered. He forces the viewer to watch and think for themselves.

Film Books You've Got To Read

Accidental Genius by Marshall Fine

A biography of John Cassavetes, who is largely credited with inventing the American Independent Film Movement. An entertaining and inspiring book that explores Cassavetes' journey, with extensive interviews with his wife Gena Rowlands and his company of cast and crew. Fortunately I discovered this book before tackling *Nightbeats* because it greatly influenced how I worked with actors, which reflects, I think, in the rich performances I was able to get.

Making Movies by Sidney Lumet

Lumet, on the other hand, approaches filmmaking from a complete 180° shift from Cassavetes' unobtrusive and freewheeling styles. His almost blue-collar approach to the work of making movies is riveting, insightful, entertaining, and a must for every filmmaker's and film lover's library.

Easy Riders, Raging Bulls and *Down And Dirty Pictures* by Peter Biskind

Two must-read books about the history and shifting tides in modern cinema. *Easy Riders, Raging Bulls* chronicles the changing of hands from the classic Hollywood studios of Daryl F. Zanuck and Jack Warner to the New Hollywood of Warren Beatty, Peter Fonda and Dennis Hopper, Francis Coppola and George Lucas, among dozens of others. *Down And Dirty Pictures* tracks the birth of the Sundance Film Festival and Miramax Pictures and the rise of the American Independent Film Movement. You must read these books to know how the American Independent Film Movement got started, how the festivals and the distribution scene has evolved, and what you might expect to happen or not happen afterwards.

When The Shooting Stops, The Cutting Begins by Ralph Rosenblum

A personal journey through the world and life of film editing by the editor of *A Thousand Clowns, The Producers,* and *Annie Hall,* for which he received the Academy Award for Best Editing. Not so much a how-to book on the intimidating process of film editing, as it is a fascinating look inside the mind of a man who so often found himself stuck as the editor on problem films where Rosenblum had the reels of film dumped in his lap and was told to make something out of it all. I love *Annie Hall,* the 88-minute Academy Award-winner for Best Picture of 1977. Until I read this book I had no idea that the film that also earned Woody Allen the Oscars for Best Director and Best Original

Screenplay (with Marshall Brickman) was originally 2½ hours long and considered unreleasable. As a result, United Artists and Woody Allen gave the film over to Rosenblum and gave him carte blanche to rethink and re-craft it into the classic that it became.

Pictures At A Revolution by Mark Harris

This is a fascinating book that looks at the making of the five films that were nominated for Best Picture of 1967: *The Graduate, Bonnie And Clyde, In The Heat Of The Night, Guess Who's Coming To Dinner* and, unbelievably, *Doctor Doolittle.* This exhaustively researched book chronicles the production life of each film from the first inception of each project, through the development and greenlighting process, casting the main players, production, editing, release strategies, all the way to the red carpet night itself. A page-turner adventure story on how movies get made the way they do.

Websites

Websites mentioned in this book:

Jimmy Bell, 3rd Bedroom Studios, Sacramento, California
3rdbedroomstudios.com

B&H Photo & Electronics Corp., New York, New York
bhphotovideo.com

Birns & Sawyer Inc.
birnsandsawyer.com

Mike Carroll, Sacramento, California
mikecarrollfilms.com
nakedfilmmaking.com

Chimera Lighting
chimeralighting.com

Alex Cox
alexcox.com

CreateSpace, self-publishing site for books, CDs and DVDs for sale on
Amazon.com
createspace.com

JEM Ball lights
jemlighting.com

Chris King, Watermark Films, Rocklin, California
watermarkfilms.net

David Lynch
davidlynch.com

Simply Scripts online source for screenplays
simplyscripts.com

Kevin Smith
kevinsmith.com

Spotted Peccary Music
spottedpeccary.com

The Studio Center, Sacramento, California
thestudiocenter.com

Withoutabox online film festival submission
withoutabox.com

Filmography

Dog Soldiers: The Dogumentary (2000)
The Garage Filmworks (mikecarrollfilms.com)
Producers: Bonnie Bennett, Mike Carroll
Director/Cinematographer/Sound/Editor: Mike Carroll
Format: Sony TRV900, Standard Definition Video, Color,
Location: New York City.
Running Rime: 44 minutes

Fish Out Of Water (2001)
Michael Dryhurst Productions
Producer/Writer/Director: Michael Dryhurst
Cinematographer/Sound/Editor: Mike Carroll
Cast: Michael Dryhurst (Morris), Victor Carosone (Al Lipski), Lillian Moncieaux (waitress), Mary Jane Popp (barmaid), Ernie Cabral (Lou), Quinn Jones-Hylton (teenager), Kim Soon Bae (Fish & Chips Owner).
Format: Sony TRV900, Standard Definition Video, Black and White, 16:9
Locations: Sacramento, Davis, California
Running Time: 8 minutes

Power (2002)
Michael Dryhurst Productions
Producer/Writer/Director: Michael Dryhurst
Cinematographer/Sound/Editor: Mike Carroll
Production Assistants: Terri Burns, Laurie Pederson, Karen Jacoby, Dominick Bernal, David Kempf, Andrea Leonard, Shawn Bockoven
Cast: Bonnie Bennett (Parnell), Jason Bortz (Dev), Carol Miranda (Consuelo), Michael Kreutzburg (Rev. Lines), Mary Jane Popp (Jessica), Jim Oliver (Bud), Jamie Coudright (Dianna), David Stickler (Trent), Eddie Madrigal (priest), Michael Kerrigan (Antiques Dealer)
Format: Sony TRV900, Standard Definition Video, Color, 16:9
Locations: San Francisco, Sacramento, El Dorado Hills, Folsom, California
Running Time: 48 minutes

Year (2006)
The Garage Filmworks (mikecarrollfilms.com)
Producers: Bonnie Bennett, Michael Dryhurst, Mike Carroll
Writer/Director/Cinematographer/Sound/Editor: Mike Carroll
Production Assistants: Dominick Bernal, Karen Olson.
Cast: Hazel R. Johnson (Doris Stone), Bonnie Bennett (Ava Stone), Christine Nicholson (Sydney Stone), Carol Miranda (Vivian Stone), Katherine Pappa (Gina Stone), Kristen Elizabeth (Lana), Savannah Swain (Chris), Blair Leatherwood (Brendan Carre), Eric Wheeler (Miles Sanders), Michael Dryhurst (Morris), Cheantell Munn (Joan), Lori Foxworth (Marcy), Kelley DuHain (Pamela), Tim Herrera (Tom), Robin Williams (DeeDee), Ted Ridgeway (David), Judy Emick (Mrs. Benjemin), Tim Herrera (Tom), Robin Williams (Deedee), Richard York (German Translator), Christa B. Brecht (German Radio Announcer)
Format: Panasonic DVX 100A, Standard Definition Video, 24p, Color, Scope 2:35
Locations: San Francisco, Sacramento, New York City, Reno, Nevada
Running Time: 109 minutes

Rachel (2008)
Watermark Films (watermarkfilms.net)
Producer/Writers: Chris & Heather King
Director/Editor: Chris King
Cinematographers: Mike Carroll (A-Camera Operator), Jason Knight (B-Camera Operator)
Sound: Jimmy Bell
Cast: Kelly Patton Nixon (Rachel), Eric Wheeler (Tom), Deborah O'Brien (Deb), Vickie Hall (Girlfriend)
Format: Panasonic DVX 100A, Standard Definition Video, 24p, Color 16:9
Location: Roseville, California.
Running Time: 13 minutes

Nightbeats (2009)

The Garage Filmworks (mikecarrollfilms.com)

Producers: Bonnie Bennett, Mike Carroll

Writer/Director/Cinematographer/Editor: Mike Carroll

Sound Design: Jimmy Bell (3rdbedroomstudios.com)

Music Consultant & Arrangements: David Blanchard

Production Assistants: Leslie Goodman, Christian Ruz Cabrera, Deanne Rotta, Jeri Hibbs, Jason Knight, Justing Taylor, Palmer Taylor, Tobija A. Annis

Cast: Lori Foxworth (Mercy), Bonnie Bennett (Edie), Kelly Patton Nixon (Cece), Anthony D'Juan (Dubois), David Harris (Nick), Francesca "Kitten" Natividad (Lola), Galen Howard (Harold), Missy Bell (Dancing Girl), Julianne Gabert (Ginger), Blair Leatherwood (Harley Sinclair), Jackie Schultz (Joline), Thom Greene (Victor), David Blanchard (pianist)

Format: JVC GY HD110U, Mini-DV cassette, High-Definition Video, 720 24p, Color 16:9

Locations: San Francisco, Sacramento, California.

Running Time: 89 minutes

Acknowledgements

This book started as a scattered collection of notes and ideas in the summer of 2007 as we were starting production on *Nightbeats*. Then I was accepted to teach a course in independent filmmaking. "Perfect," I thought. "This is going to make it much easier." In the early 70s, Jerry Lewis published *The Total Filmmaker*, a bestselling book transcribed from classes he taught at UCLA. Using this as a model, I recorded my class, figuring I could mix my notes with a transcript of the class and have a draft in a couple of months. A year later I had 130,000 rambling words, which led to another year of rewriting, editing and sifting down to the 71,000 words that remain.

Several filmmaker friends have helped me along the way, reading the various drafts, giving feedback and correcting my grammar. The language of cinema is constantly evolving, but English is far less flexible and I welcome all the help I can get. In particular, I appreciate the assistance of filmmakers Chris and Heather King, as well as Laura Chick, Deanne Rotta and Alexandra Creehan, who were in my first class.

Most significantly, I would be completely lost were it not for my wife Bonnie's many long hours reading, editing and proofing every word, comma and period on these pages. She's been at my side on the editing of the scripts and the films and has always been ready with a simple solution for how to make everything work better.

Deanne Rotta films behind-the-scenes footage on the location set of *Nightbeats* with the Sony TRV900 mini DV camcorder. Deanne took Mike Carroll's first one-man filmmaking course and is now making her own documentary as a filmmaker without a crew.

PHOTO ACKNOWLEDGEMENTS:

The behind-the-scenes photographs on the jacket and throughout the book were taken by my good friend Mike Williams, who has also been incredibly generous with his time to me over the years in guiding me through the transition into the world of Mac, for which I will be forever in his debt.

All other photos are frame blowups from the films themselves.

16096756R00151

Made in the USA
Lexington, KY
05 July 2012